The Magic Within
How To Transform Your Life

To Tom so nice to call you a friend

Alan + Cindy

Alan Wade & Cindy Preston

Copyright © 2016 by Alan Wade & Cindy Preston

Published and distributed in Canada by:
The Raymond Aaron Group,
445 Apple Creek Boulevard #122,
Markham Ontario L3R 9X7

All rights reserved. No part of this book may be reproduced by any mechanical, photographic, recording, nor may it be stored in a retrieval system, transmitted, or otherwise be copied for public or private use without prior written permission from the publisher. The intent of the authors is only to offer information of a general nature to assist in your journey of emotional and spiritual wellbeing. In the event you use any of the information in this book for yourself, which is your constitutional right, the authors and publisher assume no responsibility for your actions.

ISBN 978-1-77277-079-7

Contents

Dedication	v
Acknowledgements	vii
About the Authors	ix
Foreword	xi
Introduction	xiii
Chapter 1: You are the Magic	1
Chapter 2: My Journey of Transformation	5
Chapter 3: Transformable Adversities	15
Chapter 4: Self Care is Essential for Transforming	55
Chapter 5: Look Within - The Magic Starts Here	71
Chapter 6: Letting Go of Your Past	79
Chapter 7: Reprogram Your Mind and Release Your Inner Power	89
Chapter 8: Embracing Spiritual Practices	101
Chapter 9: Success Stories of Hope	123
Chapter 10: Learning to Be True to You	157

This Book is Dedicated

To our Creator and Higher Power,
thank you for this opportunity to serve you and others.

To our family and friends,
who have always supported us and
been there when we have needed you.

To my father, Fred Preston,
you will always be loved and cherished.
You were a loving and generous father and grandfather.
We will never forget you.
Peace be with you in heaven.

To my parents, Denis and Lucy Wade, who have been
gone for years but are not forgotten.
You instilled in me strength and courage.
To Richard, Christine, Candace, and TJ for saving me.
To my younger brother, Brian, who just passed away
June 24, 2016.
I miss the way you made me laugh, love always.

Cayla and Calyn:
Both of you have been angels in my life. I cannot even find the words to describe the unconditional and immense love that I have in my heart for you. You both have always been wise and your hearts full of love. You have grown to be the most extraordinary young adults and I could not be more proud to call you my children. You have brought a sweetness and angelic presence into my life since the day you were born. Thank you for bringing to me Paul and Alexandrea, who just add more love and happiness to our growing family. We eagerly anticipate the arrival of our newest member of the family, a new grandson. We have so much love for Kai, our first grandson, and we cannot wait to shower the new baby with the deep love that is in our hearts.
Thank you for all of the magical moments we have shared and will share in the future.
I will always love you with every beat of my heart.
Love, Mom

A very special thank you goes to the ones who have shared their stories with you in this book. It is with their help and support that this was all possible.

To those who are inspired and awakened by this book, may your journey be purposeful and full of love.

Acknowledgements

We would like to acknowledge Raymond Aaron for supporting, mentoring and assisting us in writing this book. Without Raymond, this book would not be published. We thank you from the bottom of our hearts for making our dream a reality.

A special thanks to Rosa, for your guidance, help and encouragement. Without your support, we may have never been able to complete this book.

We would like to thank the courageous people who have shared their stories in the book. It is people like you that offer hope and strength to others who are struggling with life.

Joany Gauvreau: You inspire us to follow our hearts and dreams by following yours. You are a shining light in our lives.

Carla Harmer: Your strength and courage never cease to amaze us and you exemplify unconditional love to your family and friends.

Pam Tremblay-Hayes: You are such a wise and extraordinary woman. The world needs more people like you in it.

John Hayes: You are an exceptional man and we appreciate all of your support and teachings.

Tina Pauls: We are so grateful to have you in our life. You are an angel to many people.

We would like to acknowledge our family for always being there for us and supporting us in our endeavours. We love all of you dearly.

We would like to acknowledge the spiritual teachers who share their wisdom and love with the world, may your work assist in the evolution of consciousness.

I would like to thank Alan, for supporting me through the writing of these words and being the one that encouraged me to share my story and the love in my heart with those who read this book. I love you with all of my heart.
I would like to thank Cindy, for helping on my journey of healing. With her encouragement and support, I have grown much over the last few years. I love you, beautiful sunrise.

About the Authors

Alan Wade is an author, lecturer, and seminar facilitator, who has worked in the addictions and mental health fields for years. His inspiring message assists in motivating people to create change. His lectures on addictive behaviours and relapse prevention have been well received. Alan is a Reiki practitioner and he continues to study the aboriginal culture.

Cindy Preston is an author, seminar facilitator, and lecturer, who has worked in the addictions and mental health fields as a concurrent disorders specialist. Concurrent disorders occur when an individual experiences mental health issues and addiction simultaneously. Cindy is a Reiki practitioner and she has been studying multiple forms of spirituality for many years.

From their own experiences of adversities, Alan and Cindy have used the concepts in this book to transform their lives.

They believe that you have the capacity and innate ability to heal and positively change your way of living, thus tapping into your own inner magic.

Foreword

The Magic Within is much more than just a self-help book. It is first hand experiences combined with concepts and useful strategies that you can incorporate into your life.

Alan and Cindy have shared in this book a variety of emotional experiences that they have been able to transform into something positive. Cindy explains a heartfelt incident that happened in her life and made national news. Alan and Cindy both use their own experiences within these pages to connect to you and assist you in understanding how you can transform adversities in your own life.

The information contained here is a combination of psychological and spiritual concepts that are powerful tools that you can utilize in your life to make considerable positive changes. The inner magic that Alan and Cindy describe within these pages is available to you. You are born with the ability to tap into this magic and create an incredible future for yourself.

Alan Wade & Cindy Preston

I am confident that when you read this book and follow the strategies that are easily presented, you will discover a more enriched life.

Raymond Aaron
New York Times Bestselling Author

Introduction

Alan Wade and Cindy Preston, the authors of this book, have both worked in the addictions and mental health fields for years. Alan and Cindy are practicing Reiki Masters and have studied spiritual and universal laws. They also have experienced painful and difficult times in their lives and have used the strategies that are written in this book to transform their own lives. They have written this book based on their life experiences and the professional education they have acquired through training and experience working in the field.

This book has been written to help others who are struggling in life with some painful experience or an ongoing problem that is all consuming. They are expressing to you that there is hope and that you do not have to do this alone. Many people suffer in silence for years with issues that never get resolved. This book will have explanations of different types of afflictions people may face and offer some strategies to overcome these difficulties. Take a moment and decide that you are going to change your life and improve the way you live. Living

Alan Wade & Cindy Preston

a life of peace and joy can be attained if you truly are willing to have an open mind and employ some new ways of living. Your new journey awaits!

Chapter 1

You Are The Magic

I am so excited that you have this book in your hands. You, right now, have the opportunity to do something different with your life. You can change your life. How inspiring! This is so incredible, so powerful! This moment in time is here. You created this; you are holding this book in your hands. Feel the excitement; your life can change for the better! All that it takes is a decision, so decide that you can do this. Now let's begin to tap into the magic within. Yes, the magic is within you!

You hold the key to your inner magic. This is very important for you to understand. If you want to change your life for the better, then you have to take your power back! You are way more powerful then you realize, more than you can imagine. You have an unmistakable inner power that resides inside of you, which you can ignite. This is your true essence, the real you that is perfect and unlimited. When you realize that you can use your mind as a tool and make it work for you, then you can change your life. As we move throughout this book, we will be sharing with you some strategies and ideas that you can employ to start making positive changes. It starts with one decision, and you have the power to make that decision.

This means that you stop blaming others for everything that has happened in your life and start realizing that you are responsible for you and the choices that you make.

This is a hard pill to swallow for many people, because they then have to look at themselves and the mistakes they have made. This sometimes causes people to feel guilty and sad for their past choices. A great way to overcome this issue is to ask yourself, "What did I learn from this and how can I do it different in the future?" Every circumstance in life has a gem hidden in it. We just have to take the time to find it. When you learn from your mistakes, instead of hiding from them, you take your power back and realize that you can change your life!

The next issue that many people face is the resistance to becoming responsible for yourself and your life. Many people have a victim mindset. This mindset is the result of a belief that says, "I am a victim of life's circumstances." Due to this belief, you will find yourself being a victim time and time again. If you are feeling resistance to the idea of becoming responsible, then you may have a victim mentality. If you are one of these people, then I challenge you to ask yourself, "What is my payoff?" If you take the time to think about this honestly, you may be surprised to find the answer to this question. Everything that you do has a payoff or you would stop doing it. Once you figure this out, then you may want to explore the alternatives and find a healthier way to meet that need or decide that this behaviour is no longer serving you.

I have found in life that when I have struggled with a situation that it often ended up being a blessing in disguise. At the time I wondered, why is this happening to me? Then after some time had passed, I realized that the situation worked out perfectly for my best interests. I am sure if you look back on your life, you will also see many things that you are now grateful that they happened.

The next chapter will describe a life-changing situation that I have endured, which completely traumatized my whole family. This event ended up becoming national news. As a result, it increased the pain and suffering of my family, while leaving the reputation of my father infamous to the public.

I hope that sharing my experience with you will assist in your own journey to transforming the painful adversities in your life. I will be sharing with you from the pain that stung deep into my heart, the same heart that beats today with gratitude and love. I acknowledge that many of you who read this book have also experienced heart-wrenching pain and you may be looking for some solace and peace. I thank you for taking the time to learn and grow by reading this book. My belief is that if we support each other and learn to love in the face of pain that we can conquer the shadows and darkness that have overcast our lives.

Chapter 2

My Journey of Transformation

On March 8, 2010, the scent of coffee was in the air, a typical morning in our home. We waited patiently for our morning java to brew. Finally, the taste of morning dew poured into our cups and we sighed as we sipped from the warm pleasure. The phone rang and it was my father. Relieved to hear his voice, I said, "Dad, where are you? I have been worried all night." My Dad replied that he was at my aunt's house and he was looking for my mother. I told him that I did not know of my mother's whereabouts. He replied, "Find her and have her call me back at her sister's house." I told him that I was not sure if I could do that and he just repeated to me to have Mom call him and hung up. I was concerned, as this was not my father's usual behaviour. I talked to my family about the phone call. We decided that we would call him back and tell him that we couldn't find Mom and ask him to come home. My father had been struggling with the recent separation from my mother. Due to this, he was constantly trying to make contact with her. My sister, Anne called him back and gave him the message, but she also told him to come home to people who loved him, as he had been very sad about his life. He would not accept our answer, and urged us to find Mom. He was not himself, so she started questioning him in regard to why he was at our aunt's and that she wanted to speak to her. He replied, "She is not here and I am not sure where she is." He stated that he was planning to visit her for a few days and also meet up with a friend. Anne tried to console him and again urged him to come home. She asked, "What is going on Dad?" He paused, appearing apathetic and unresponsive. He replied, "Thank you, but I have nothing left to live for," and hung up.

We decided to call the police because we were very worried about the state of his mental health. We urged them to have him picked up for a psychological evaluation. The police asked if my Dad had guns. We replied, "Yes." My Dad was a talented and avid hunter. The police assured us that they would keep in touch with us in regard to my Dad's status.

Time crawled by slowly as we anguished over our Dad's whereabouts.

Tears flowed down my face, as I had a gut feeling that something was dreadfully wrong. Anne said to me, "I think that is the last time that I will ever speak to Dad."

At 3:30pm, the phone rang. It was the police asking us to come to the station with all of the registered guns that were in the gun cabinet. When we arrived, we were greeted and taken into a private room. Three police officers came into the room and informed us that our father had been in a shootout with a police officer and the officer was in critical condition. When we asked about Dad, they told us that he was injured, but none of his injuries was life threatening.

We burst into tears and held each other in shock and disbelief. We asked questions and cried uncontrollably. We were then asked for statements. In shock and devastated, we reluctantly agreed. We each took turns trying to maintain composure just minutes after hearing the tragic news of our beloved father. The questions were grueling and very painful as we tried to remember the days leading up to this horror in our lives.

Then we received the most devastating news that rocked our very core.

The police informed us that the officer that was injured by our Dad had died and that our Dad was having surgery in the hospital with non-life threatening injuries. We begged to see our father so we could support him and talk to him about this horrifying event. The police denied our request. Our hearts were crushed and we wailed in pain and sorrow. The police charged our Dad with shooting and killing a police officer. Our loving, hardworking, elderly father would spend the remainder of his life in prison.

The most confusing part for us was the fact that our Dad had lived a life of obeying the law. He was a Christian who committed his life to his church and his beliefs. He was active in politics and he acted as reeve for years in the township of Joly. He was a good father and grandfather. He would give you the shirt off of his back, because he was generous to a fault. So how could this have happened?

We returned home in disbelief. I paced back and forth, wracking my brain as to how this could have happened. I could not grasp how my Dad could perform such an act. My heart ached thinking that I could not see him in his intense time of need. Sobbing took over and I fell to the floor, surrendering to the pain within my heart.

The phone rang; it was one of my cousins. He told me how sorry he was for this event, and then he offered the services of his attorney to assist with my Dad. What a miracle and an amazing gift, as we did not have the money to hire a lawyer. We immediately called the lawyer and asked how we could see our Dad. He told us to call the CEO of the hospital that he was admitted to for surgery. The CEO can override the decision of the police. We made the phone call and we were approved to see our Dad.

Relieved, we packed and drove to London to see our precious father, picking up our family along the way.

When we arrived at the hospital we were informed that our Dad had endured multiple gunshot wounds including one to his head. Some of the bullets were still in his body and he was in a coma. After hearing this information, we were in shock because we were told previously that he had non-life threatening injuries. After consulting with doctors we were finally permitted to see him. We went in groups of two due to them only allowing us to visit in small numbers.

We told Dad that we loved him unconditionally. We reminded him of how he was a wonderful father and grandfather and that he had lived a life of love and generosity. Even though he had been involved in this tragic incident, we still were at his side and supporting him with our love.

We spent the next few days meeting with doctors and nurses and having family meetings, trying to make the best-informed decision for our precious father. After much painstaking thought, we decided to take him off of his life support. We decided to let God decide if our Dad lived or surrender to his injuries.

We surrounded him and spent our last moments with our Dad. During those precious moments, we held his hand, stroked him, prayed for him, sang him his favourite hymns and told him that if he chose to leave that we were ready to support him in moving to the spirit world. He died 45 minutes later.

Driving home, we were in shock and pain. We never thought that we would ever have to experience this kind of trauma in our lives. We thought that the drama was over. It was just beginning!

Media followed us. They came to our homes, and called us incessantly asking for interviews. At this point, we were exhausted and overwhelmed. We wanted to just heal from this horrific event. The days that followed were a roller coaster of emotions. I felt numb most of the time as we made arrangements for the funeral and avoided the media. The pain in my heart was unbearable at times and I would sob uncontrollably. Thank God, I had my family with me for mutual support. We would go into my Dad's room and put on some of his clothes and immerse ourselves in his aroma. We would lay on his bed and take in the energy that lingered in our memories. My Dad spent most of his life working in the bush as a lumberjack and, in his spare time, he would carve animals from wood. He often would have a sweet scent of freshly cut trees and shavings of wood on his clothes.

The small community that we lived in was incredibly helpful; people brought us meals and heartfelt support. My Dad was well known in town as a good man and everyone was in shock and disbelief.

The funeral was therapeutic, having so many people visit and sharing their condolences.

After the funeral, my new reality set in. I experienced a myriad of emotions that would surface like waves, retreat and then return again. Sometimes numbness would overcome my body and I would get some relief for a period of time. However, it was short lived and reality would hit me like a ton of bricks. Literally, it would hit me and the pain would weigh me down. Sometimes I felt so heavy, walking seemed like a chore. The weight of sadness overcame me some days and I wondered if I would ever feel "normal" again.

As time went on, we have learned more about the incident with my Dad. First of all, we have found out that my Dad shot at the officer's hand. Due to that shot, the officer's gun flew apart. Debris from the gun flew into his head, causing the damage that resulted in him passing on. When thinking about it, my Dad was very talented at shooting guns from his hunting days. If he had wanted the officer to die, he would have shot him and he would have died immediately. So my question is why did he shoot his hand? I don't think that he had any intention of killing him. We also found out from the autopsy that my Dad was experiencing the early stages of Alzheimer's disease, which includes forgetfulness, as well as mood and behavioural changes.

Dad also had a couple of incidents where he would have lapses of complete memory loss. He would not know where or who he was, and this would go on for hours. He had diabetes, which also affects mood and other physical issues that could have been a precursor to his behaviours. I also know that he was suffering from symptoms of depression and anxiety without treatment. All of these issues combined may have contributed to his behaviour in his last moments. However, we will never know what really happened. All that I do know is that my Dad was not the man depicted in the media. He was a man who had worked very hard to care for his family, and he was committed to his community and church. If an animal was wounded or abandoned, he would care for it. He would help out anyone he could who was less fortunate. He had a heart of gold and he was sensitive to the suffering of others.

Due to overwhelming circumstances my Dad lost his way, he forgot who he truly was and this led to a traumatic death for him and the officer.

A message to my Dad:

You are free, you are love,
you are loved, you will always
BE

I will continue to share my experience throughout this book and what I did to move through my grief. After some time passed, I asked myself, "Do I want this to make me bitter or better?" I chose better and I hope that you do as well!

Chapter 3

Transformable Adversities

Stress

After the death of my father, stress became very familiar to me. My whole life had changed and I was still in shock and overwhelmed by the whole experience. As a family, we did our best to assist each other, but the pain in our hearts was raw. I took some time off of work to heal my heart. Due to the nature of my work as a therapist, I had to make sure that I was well enough to be a counsellor to my clients. I ended up taking a vacation with some of my family members to help with my healing. We went to Florida to soak up the sun and sink our feet into the sand near the ocean, simply to enjoy being away from the drama of home. I made notes of my thoughts about the horrifying event that I just endured. This was a great way to deal with the stress that I was experiencing. I returned home in a better place. Unfortunately, my marriage dissolved and my finances were at the brink of disaster. Stress was again at an all-time high for me and I did not know which way to turn. I am so grateful that my sister was living with me at the time. Her tenderness and love helped me to heal. She is a Reiki Master as well, and we would take turns giving each other treatments. Annette would constantly assure me that my life would get better and that I was a wonderful woman. As time went forward, her words started to resonate with me and I started to feel better. We both loved to dance, so we went to our belly dance classes regularly and performed when possible to bring back some joy into our lives.

Stress is not always a negative thing. Sometimes it is necessary to make positive changes in our lives. It is your response to stress that determines the impact that stress will have on you. When your brain perceives stress, it may signal the fight or flight response. This is a biochemical change that assists you in dealing with perceived danger. Symptoms, such as increased heart rate, acute vision and hearing, can be experienced. This response is appropriate when you are in a situation where you have to fight for your life. However, if it happens too often from perceived stress and life in general, stress can have adverse consequences. In my experience, ongoing stress has caused digestion problems, a decrease in my immune system, migraine headaches and led to depression.

Here are some tools that have helped me in my life:

Relaxation:
In my experience, learning to relax has been very beneficial to decreasing stress.

Your body and brain work together. Once your mind recognizes that you are no longer in danger, the stress response will turn off. I often offer my clients a strategy to use to help with this. I encourage them to take slow, deep, long breaths, breathing with their stomach, coupled with self-talk, such as saying, "I am safe. Right now, I am okay." This works to calm the mind and the body at the same time. More of this will be discussed in the self-care chapter.

Analyzing the stressful situation:
I have found that taking some time to think about what is causing stress for me and then considering how I can make some changes to alleviate it has also helped.

Example:
Always being late for work.

You can change this issue easily by getting up earlier and reducing the stress of rushing around.

Sometimes you have stress that you cannot change, like the traffic on the way to work. However, you can change the way you react to it by coming up with strategies to alter your perception. This could mean listening to a book download, or your favourite music, or just taking that time to be with yourself and think about your future goals.

A major component of my stress relief is sometimes just accepting the fact that some things are not going to change. Once I accept the fact that I cannot change the situation at this time, it relieves my mind of searching for ways to overcome the situation.

Asking for help:
I have found that stress occurs for me when I try to do everything myself. The result of this has left me drained and exhausted. Delegating and asking someone for help is a win-win situation. The worst thing that can happen is that they will say no, and if they do, then I can ask someone else. When you ask someone for help, it may offer him or her a gift of feeling helpful and important.

Time out:
Taking time out for myself has been one of my major sources of stress relief. Having a day to just be quiet, read a book, go to the beach, have lunch with a friend, watch

funny movies, and exercise. There are so many things that you can do to take time for yourself. This is essential to relieving stress and rejuvenating your soul.

Meditation:
Meditation has been a lifesaver for me. When I am stressed out and life seems overwhelming, I meditate. There are many types of meditation. I am going to go into more detail regarding meditation in later chapters.

Exercise:
I love to dance. All I have to do is put on music and my body automatically wants to move. It is freeing for me and I forget about what is upsetting me. Also, exercise keeps you healthy and it changes the chemicals in your brain. Daily exercise will also decrease anxiety and depression. This is a great natural way to de-stress.

Supportive friends:
Having a healthy support system in my life is imperative. I am so grateful for the absolutely incredible friends that I have. There have been many times when I needed my friends to help me through difficult situations. Your support can be friends, co-workers, support groups, and if necessary, find a good therapist to assist you with stress. I am so blessed to have amazing friends who are there for

me when I am struggling. I ask them to send me light and they all know that I need some love and good energy. They will also call me or visit me to check in. Recently, I have been struggling with a situation in my life that had consumed me. I was struggling to get myself centered again, even though I knew what to do. I needed the aid of my friends to help me move forward. The assistance that was given to me has been incredible. I have since then been able to transform my perception, thus changing the course of my life. I realized that sometimes I need help and I ask for it. We end up becoming closer, plus we all learn something from the experience.

Laughter:
There have been times when I have rented or watched a funny movie to help me de-stress. Laughter is the best medicine. Do something fun, play with your dog, sing and dance around your house, or hang out with children. They remind us to live in the moment.

Attitude:
There have been times when my attitude needed a huge adjustment. Once I changed my attitude, my stress would immediately decrease. Attitude is paramount to perception. The way we perceive the world is the key to

our reaction/response, which can result in stress reduction.

Self-talk:
When I paid attention to my self-talk, I would realize that I was creating my own stress. Self-talk is imperative to reduce stress. There have been times in the past when I would berate myself mercilessly. I had a friend who would say to me, "Put the stick down, Cindy." At first I thought, "What?" But then I realized that I was beating myself up. No wonder I was stressed; I did it to myself. That led me to start paying attention to my thoughts.

Negative thoughts:
Once I started paying attention to my thoughts, I identified that I had been reliving negative situations over and over in my mind. I was constantly worrying about something that could happen to me in the future. The good thing was that I had control over this, because I was doing this to myself. Now I could make some changes. It was much easier said than done, but I was determined to transform this way of thinking. And in time, I did.

Stay tuned, because we are going to talk about this more as well.

To summarize, stress can be difficult sometimes. However, we can do some self-care to assist with our reactions to stress. Breathing and self-talk are critical, but it is also important to exercise, laugh and let things go.

Grief:
After the death of my father, I was paralyzed by grief. I felt heavy and sadness overcame my heart and soul. I had never lost a person to death and this death was so tragic. I felt a myriad of feelings daily, but most frequently I felt sadness. I decided to allow myself to feel my feelings, as I did not want to get stuck in my grief. Many people just try to avoid their feelings by working all the time, substance use/abuse, denial, cleaning, shopping and the list goes on and on. While they think it is helping them cope, all that this does is keep you stuck in the grief, and you don't move forward. It sucks because the feelings are uncomfortable, but worth it. It takes courage to feel your grief and allow yourself to let the feelings move through you. I had days of anger, sadness, denial, guilt, self-blame, severe heartache, and eventually acceptance, but that took a lot of time. These are the stages of grief that are experienced during moments of the grieving period. Elizabeth Kubler Ross wrote a book about grief, called *On Death and Dying*. Through the years, I have used her concepts when working with clients to assist in their grieving process.

It is important to honour your feelings, so that you can work through the grief. I had days when I was really angry at the situation and I wanted answers. I would research things and talk to people about what happened. I was very angry with the police for a while. I wanted to call the media and give them a piece of my mind for writing lies about my Dad to the world. I desperately wanted the world to know that my Dad was not a monster! He was my Dad, he loved me all of my life, he protected me from danger, and worked in adverse temperatures to keep me fed and warm. He rocked me to sleep. No, he was not perfect. He had his faults, but he was not the man depicted in the media. I decided that I would not let this harden me. I lived in a small town most of my life. I knew some police officers and they were wonderful people. I had to accept the situation to have peace in my heart.

At some point, everyone will experience grief. Grief is not just about death. It can be a divorce, loss of a job, health challenges, or even the loss of your favourite coping mechanism (alcohol). Yes, people grieve the substance that they no longer have as a coping mechanism. This is a big issue that gets addressed in treatment. Grief is a loss of something that you enjoyed or needed in your life. It is so important to allow yourself to feel and move through the grief. If it becomes overwhelming, talk to someone, see a counsellor, or attend a grief group. You don't have to do this alone. You are not alone.

I would say that the most beneficial thing that assisted me in my grief was my spirituality. I have leaned on my spirituality many times in my life. This time, it was my saving grace. I meditated, I spent time in nature, I got Reiki treatments, spent time with supportive people, cuddled with my dogs, and I prayed. I always knew that my Dad was with me. Even though it was hard, my spirit knew that he was there comforting me, and helping me get through the most difficult time in my life.

Blaming:
After my father's death, I blamed the police and myself for his death for a period of time. These behaviours did not serve me, and it actually caused me to stay stuck in my grief. I blamed myself for calling the police when I was worried about him. I felt that if I had not called them, then he may have lived and the officer may also be alive. This haunted me for a few years after his death. I would go over the situation in my mind, trying to make sense of it and trying to come up with a better outcome. I could never get past it. I also blamed the police. I thought that if they had taken our concerns more seriously about his mental health condition, maybe the situation could have been prevented

all together. However, I finally realized that I could not go back in time and change any of it. I needed to let it go. As time went by, I forgave the police and myself. Ironically, the inquest was a healing time for me, as I met some of the officers and the deceased officer's family. I realized that everyone was just doing the best that they could in a terrible situation. My heart had compassion for them. I also admired the deceased officer's family for the faith and love that they emanated.

I have found myself blaming outside circumstances many times in my life. It was a way to avoid taking responsibility for the way my life had turned out. Blaming does not serve you in the end. The result of blaming is not learning from your mistakes and staying stuck in your pain.

Have you ever asked yourself, "Why does my life suck?" Did you ever think, "Was I born this way? If only I got a break in life, but I am unlucky." Can you think of people or institutions that are to blame for your lot in life? You have to take responsibility for the way your life is, because you are the one that got yourself to where you are at this moment. It was your choices based on the circumstances you were presented with. When a person is constantly blaming outside circumstances for their life, then they don't open themselves up to the possibilities of personal growth. This is how you sell yourself short. You end up keeping yourself as a victim, limiting yourself unnecessarily. "Poor me" is the message you give others. The first step to changing this behaviour is to start taking ownership for your actions. Once you make the decision to learn from your mistakes, you will then take your life in a new direction. Learning and growing from mistakes will lead to positive outcomes.

Anger:
For some reason, I received the message during my life to repress my anger. Through my training, I learned how damaging that could be. I have experienced depression, due in part to turning my anger inward. I would blame myself for things that sometimes I was not even responsible for. I had a difficult time admitting that I was angry with other people and denied my anger. This led to dysfunction in my relationships and my own suffering. After my Dad died, I allowed myself to feel the anger and it helped me to take action when necessary. However, I had to be careful at times, because the anger became very strong and I did not want to act out inappropriately. This happened when the media would hound my family, and especially when they showed up at my Dad's funeral. I had to take a deep breath and tell myself to calm down, because it was not worth getting upset over.

There is healthy and unhealthy anger.

Healthy anger allows us to make sure that we are not being taken advantage of. I think of anger as a feeling, not good or bad. It is my body's way of telling me something is wrong, pay attention. When a person deals with anger in a healthy way, they may take some time out, go for a walk, journal, breathe slowly, or talk to a friend. Taking time to think about the situation and then acting in a safe and effective manner is a way to express healthy anger. Talking to the person that you are angry with in a calm manner or deciding to change the way you perceive the situation are two healthy approaches.

Talking it out in a safe effective manner is very helpful in relationships. It assists in continuing with healthy communication.

Unhealthy anger can be an irrational response to a situation. This state of mind will decrease a person's logic. It is a reaction to circumstances and the reaction may result in physical or emotional abuse. Unhealthy anger may sometimes lead to the inability to maintain control, resulting in destructive behaviours for yourself and others. Holding onto anger causes health issues, emotional dysfunction and is the root cause of resentments. It can eat you up and keep you as a hostage to an unhealthy lifestyle.

Part of letting go of anger is dealing with your resentments. Holding resentments is like allowing poison to stay in your body and make you sick. Resentments are prevalent in addictions. If a person does not address their resentments, they may find themselves in the relapse cycle. This occurs when a person holds onto anger toward another person or event. Eventually, it eats at them until something happens, such as getting sick physically or mentally. To address resentments, a person will need to employ an attitude of forgiveness. This is not to condone the other person's actions; it is to release them from the prison that they have created in their own mind. In my experience, there were many times I had been in denial of my resentments. Yet, sometimes my resentments were focused toward myself.

Recently, I was home sick from a stomach flu and I was lying in bed meditating about being sick. I realized that I was holding onto anger toward a past partner. I was shocked at this message and was thinking; I am not an angry person. After some reflection, I realized that I was very angry with that person and that I had been carrying the anger inside my body. I decided to forgive them and did a meditation on forgiveness towards them. I knew when the anger left because I instantly felt the pain leave my stomach. I was in shock and disbelief. I had just witnessed how toxic anger and resentment could make me sick. I am so grateful that I no longer hold that toxic anger/resentment inside my body.

Anger can be a learned behaviour from parents or authority figures. In abusive families, anger can be learned and is used as a way to intimidate others.

Some people repress their anger and this can also lead to health and emotional issues. These people will deny they are angry, but the anger is oozing from every pore. Depression can be a result of anger turned inward. In this case, the person will turn their anger onto themselves, leading them to self-hatred. This can cause many psychological conditions.

Here are a few ways you can deal with unhealthy anger. First of all, admit that you are angry and allow yourself to feel the anger in a safe and healthy way. Go take some time out and think about the situation, cool down and then decide what the appropriate thing is for you to do. One of the most important things to learn is assertiveness, so that you can articulate your needs in a safe way and not blame the other person. An example of this would be to make a statement such as: I feel angry when you don't treat me with respect. I would appreciate it if you considered my feelings when you speak to me. This example uses "I" statements. When you use "I" statements, then you take responsibility for your feelings and translate your needs to the other person in a win-win situation. When a person starts a sentence with "you", the other person instantly feels like they are being attacked, so they become defensive. This leaves both people in a non-constructive situation.

Using "I" statements takes some practice. Start out using them in situations that are not emotionally charged. Therefore, don't practice on your partner or someone who you have a difficult relationship with. Try it at a restaurant when your food is cold or some situation that is not heated.

If you have unresolved anger that you find just under the surface, ready to explode, then you may want to seek counsel from a therapist. Sometimes this type of explosive anger requires more assistance than assertiveness and using time out strategies.

Shame & Guilt:
I have found during my years working as a therapist that many people have a difficult time distinguishing the

difference between shame and guilt. The way I explain it to my clients is:

Guilt means I have made mistakes.
Shame means I am a mistake.
-Terry Gorski (1988)

There is a huge difference between these two issues.

Guilt is much easier to overcome, because it is a negative feeling about a behaviour you engaged in. You realize that you made a mistake, but you are still a worthwhile person. When we feel guilty, we desire for atonement or to make amends. You can learn from mistakes you have made, making new choices in the future. I often tell my clients, "You can't change the past, but you can change the future." Instead of living in guilt, you can move forward and know that you are now making choices that empower you. Guilt only keeps you stuck in the past.

Shame, on the other hand, is a deep feeling that lives inside you and penetrates your soul. It is a painful, dreadful feeling of emptiness from your core. It can manifest in behaviours, such as perfectionism, self-doubt, and sometimes paranoia. Shame can result in feelings of inferiority, failure, inadequacy, humiliation and worthlessness.

What brings about shame? Circumstances ranging from family secrets, trauma, cultural identification and messages you received during your life. With these messages, a person may take on shame that was given to them by someone else. I can relate to this, as I was shamed as a child by authoritative people who were emotionally abusive toward me. When I examined this, I realized that the messages given to me were not true. I let them go, released them and the shame diminished. That was not my shame to carry any longer.

Shame is common in families with addictions. The chemical dependent person feels ashamed because they cannot control their use of substances. Family members experience shame as well. People who experience shame have an external locus of control, meaning that they constantly seek outside validation from others. This leads to feeling helpless in the face of the mood and attitude of other people in their life. The person then strives harder to appease others for approval. It becomes a vicious cycle of pain and dysfunction. The shamed person strives for constant control in relationships in order to keep that status quo. This leads to unhealthy behaviours, such as abuse, intimidation, seduction, people pleasing and care-taking. Denial keeps them bound to this cycle of pain and desperation. You can overcome shame, but it is a process that takes time, patience and learning to love yourself.

Some strategies that have worked for me are:
Be willing to be vigorously honest to yourself and others. I found that the person that I lied to the most was myself. It was mostly out of denial. I was not ready to deal with my reality at that time in my life. I now work hard at being more aware of what is really going on and use the support in my life to work through what I am experiencing.

State your truth in an assertive and calm manner. I have found that stating and owning my truth has helped me to become more assertive and find assistance in getting my needs met.

Attend counselling and self-help support groups to ensure personal growth.

I have dedicated my life to constant personal growth and improvement. By committing to this, I have to be open to learn new things about new concepts and myself.

Self-care has been critical, in my experience, to overcoming shame. A person with shame does not think that they deserve self-care, because it goes against their grain. Do it anyway and learn to become your own best friend.

Again, becoming aware of self-talk and maintaining a new way of life helps with shame, as your thoughts are powerful in transformation and healing. I practiced positive affirmations daily, such as "I am a good person." This was incremental in my healing process.

Gradually change your affirmations to ones that you can use to transform how you think and your beliefs about yourself, such as, "I am an amazing and strong woman/man."

Healing shame takes time to learn to love the inner child inside you, which is yearning for love and acceptance. The inner child work that I did was transforming for me in regards to healing shame. I did some work on my inner child through meditation. I found some John Bradshaw tapes and I followed his instructions for inner child work. I spent time with my inner child and told her that I will always be there from now on to love and protect her. This work was tremendous in my healing.

I would give my clients, who had some problems with shame, very specific homework. I would tell them to think of someone in their life that they love with all of their heart, such as a child or pet. For the next week, they had to treat themselves as they would that person/thing that they love. If they would not say or do something to that person/thing that they love, then they cannot do it to themselves. This helps to put you on the journey to self-love and acceptance.

Addictions:
Addiction can show up in many forms, such as substance use, gambling, sex, exercise, food, shopping and more. This disease can manifest in people in all walks of life, from a teacher, pilot, doctor, counsellor, server, or dentist. This disease leaves the addict spinning out of control and the people in their lives feeling desperate and alone. The chemically dependent person is affected biologically, psychologically, socially and spirituality. In order for the chemically dependent person to heal, they have to address these four areas. Addiction is a family disease; no one in the family escapes the dysfunction and pain. Unfortunately, this is a disease of denial, so everyone is running around ignoring how this is adversely affecting his or her life. In some families, it continues for generations. For some, they can break the cycle and have positive change. My way of describing the difference

between someone dealing with substance abuse and addiction is that addiction takes away your choice. Someone who has an addiction can no longer control his or her use of substances. The substance/addiction takes control of them. It is like the person no longer holds a bottle of alcohol in their hand. Instead, they live in the bottle. This leads to shame and guilt in an ongoing cycle of pain that the addict endures on a daily basis. The pain from withdrawal and the adverse consequences of years of abuse and emotional suffering keeps the victim in a cycle they can't break without help. When an addict uses substances, life becomes unmanageable, resulting in negative consequences from their substance use. Even though their lives have become very difficult and chaos is all around them, they continue to use substances. Consequences continue to add up and they feel trapped in a cycle of hell. However, help is available for you to get your life back.

For the chemically dependent person, there is treatment. Residential treatment is recommended, as it is like putting a foundation under a house. These facilities assist the person in addressing the thoughts and behaviours at the root of the disease. Yes, putting the plug in the jug is literally the first step. The work has just begun. If a person stops using substances, they may experience withdrawal symptoms. These symptoms can range in complexity and intensity depending on the substance they use.

It is important to go to a detoxification unit or hospital if symptoms become severe, as some withdrawal symptoms can be life threatening. Alcohol withdrawal can be a risk, if a person has drank daily and excessively for many years. Consult your doctor or an addiction expert, before you attempt to withdraw from substances.

Residential treatment will address underlying issues; substance abuse is a symptom of the disease. AA and self-help meetings are very beneficial as support. Having a sponsor is essential for a person's recovery to provide a touchstone through these major changes. A person in recovery has to change everything in his/her life. It is like learning to live again without the substance as a coping mechanism. I am focusing here on substances, but for any addiction the treatment is essentially the same, just a different coping mechanism.

The disease of addiction is very baffling. The addict craves instant gratification and the thirst for substances becomes insatiable. Ravenous cravings can become a curse that will drive the individual toward indulgence. This is very difficult to overcome on your own. The support from a counsellor and community is beneficial for a healthy recovery. Core issues need to be addressed to ensure a successful and happy life of sobriety. If these issues are not addressed, then the dry drunk syndrome may emerge. Feelings of deprivation may manifest. Serenity will be severed and discontent will take on a new form. Reaching out is the lifeline for recovery. Having someone to hold you accountable to is of utmost importance. Addiction is a disease of denial. Slipping back into old patterns happens without you realizing it. A mentor/sponsor will guide you and help you to avoid relapse. When you begin your journey of sobriety, it is important to have a social life with sober people. These people will understand you and also recognize when you are slipping back into old patterns. You have suffered enough and you are worth the effort to change your life. It does not matter what you have or have not done, you are worthy of a good life. Don't wait one more minute to call a local addiction agency, or go to an AA meeting. Do whatever it takes to get your life back. You can do this!

Addiction Related Issues & Co-Dependency:
It is important to understand that addiction affects the whole family. This includes everyone who has regular contact with the addictive person. The family members will take on roles to adjust to the dysfunction they live

with. The chief enabler is usually the spouse, due to the fact that denial runs rampant with this disease. If the chemical dependent is a child, then the parents are the chief enablers. This may sound crazy, as the family only wants the addict to stop using. However, due to the nature of the disease and how people react, they end up becoming the major enablers in that person's life. The whole family has to get help, otherwise the pattern will continue forward. Many times I have seen the chemical dependent person go to treatment and when they return home, the conflict with their partner is so destructive that they end up separating. This could be prevented if the spouse and family members would meet with the counsellor and chemical dependent as part of the treatment, so that they can all work as a team to succeed. The family members would also benefit from some co-dependency counselling to ensure their own recovery. Many times the partner is so angry and hurt that they do not want to participate in any education or support. Looking at them is not a priority, as they believe that they do not have the problem. Unfortunately, they do not realize that they need the assistance as much as the addict in their lives.

Sadly, many people are not open to help and they continue to repeat the same defeating behaviours associated with substance related issues.

The addict also needs to address these behaviours, as they also have co-dependency traits that are underlying.

Co-Dependency:
This is also a disease that permeates a person's ability to love themselves. The person who experiences co-dependency has difficulty honouring their own feelings or even admitting that they have feelings. They put others first, at the expense of losing their identity and emotional health. They feel frustrated, alone and desperate to be acknowledged.

Depression and anxiety may take over, and they feel powerless to change their lives. Co-dependency does not always stem from a home of substance abuse. It can result from living with a person with mental or physical illness, where you have to put your needs on the back burner. Also, it can result from living in a religious family, where the person receives messages that others come first at the expense of their own wellbeing.

The individual who engages in these behaviours spends his/her life feeling exhausted, overwhelmed and angry, but they don't know why. The anger may turn inward and result in depression. Anxiety is also a symptom, due to the individual caring so much about what other people think of them, in that they become overly involved in trying to keep the status quo of appearing "normal".

People pleasing becomes paramount. You end up putting your self-esteem in the hands of others and leaving yourself helpless to your own opinion of self-worth. The individual has a false belief that they, in some way, can control others. They spend a lot of energy trying to figure out how to control other people's opinions of them. This results in much turmoil in relationships, as others resent being controlled, therefore creating conflict. The individual's self-esteem and self-worth decreases leaving them feeling unworthy and undeserving of anything good. Chronic shame becomes a familiar feeling that drives the dysfunctional behaviour.

I have struggled with co-dependency for most of my life. It has affected my relationships in a negative way and left me feeling depressed and hopeless. Since my training, I have worked on it considerably. However, I have to keep tabs on it, as co-dependency creeps up and bites me in the butt on occasion. It is helpful to have someone in your life that can help keep you accountable for your behaviours.

Here are some traits that I experienced with co-dependency. If you find that you identify with some of these, then it is the beginning of becoming aware of behaviours that are no longer serving you. Do not beat yourself up if you do identify with these examples. Awareness is the first step to change.

I have found that being a mother has been the most satisfying experience. However, I had to examine my behaviours when it came to my children, because I would always rescue them. I became aware that it could create dependency with them and others. I would try to fix other people and rescue them from the consequences of lessons that may have been life changing for them. I also realized that it is a way of saying, "Let me do it for you, because you are not capable."

As my children grew, I had to learn how to identify and take care of my own needs and allow them to learn to take care of their lives. Always controlling the outcome of their actions kept them from learning. I have learned to check in with myself and take care of my needs first. I realize now that I am worth taking care of. I will always be there for my grown children. Yet, I am also aware of my needs and the importance of allowing them to take charge of their own lives.

I found that I would feel responsible for other people. This again is not helpful for the people in your life. It is difficult for many people to understand that we cannot control others, especially their mood or feelings. It is important to allow others to feel their feelings and to work through their own pain. Once I realized this, it was like a weight was lifted off of me.

I was also seeking the approval of other people. Needing the approval of others left me in a situation where I gave control over to them, and it left me powerless to others.

One of the biggest things that I had to learn was to say "no." Many times I would get myself into situations that I did not want to be in due to not being able to say "NO." Now I listen to my gut and I have learned to say no politely and without guilt. This is a huge issue for some people. I actually have given my clients a paper with NO written on it and tell them to put it on their fridge and read it out loud when they pass by it.

Saying "yes" when you mean "no" will only defy yourself and leave you feeling angry and sad. I often teach people to start listening to their gut and when it is screaming NOOOO, listen to it and act accordingly. Our gut, a sixth sense that is always communicating with us, is important to listen to.

I used to believe that I was not allowed to make others angry; therefore I lived in a constant state of fear. I was so fearful of being alone that I would do whatever it took to make others happy. I would wear a mask of, "I am okay," but underneath I was falling apart. I never got my needs met, because I didn't think that I had the right to ask. As a result, I gave my power away. I desperately hoped that others would figure out what my needs were and I ended up disappointed. As a result, I ended up with aggressive partners, due to the fact that I had difficulty asserting my own rights. Unfortunately, I ended up living as a victim.

I found that for me the key to overcoming this trait was to realize that I am important. I started saying affirmations, and as time went on, I started to believe them. I learned assertive communication skills that assisted in getting my needs met. I became responsible for me and I learned to love me.

I spent many years living with a martyr mentality. This was a faulty belief system. I felt like I had to sacrifice myself and suffer due to my religious upbringing. Being a martyr made me fearful of good things happening to me. Often I would sabotage any good that came into my life. The self-prophesying beliefs that I employed became my reality. Self-prophesying beliefs are deeply ingrained beliefs, which end up manifesting in our lives. As I said earlier, you are very powerful. I will talk about this later on in the book. I believed that life is supposed to be a struggle, so I created suffering in my life. This caused anxiety, as I was always waiting for the other shoe to drop. Enjoying life and having fun was foreign to me.

In recovery from this mentality, I became aware that it is important to realize that I didn't need to struggle or suffer in life and it is okay to let go of being the victim. Again affirmations are helpful for this on a daily basis, such as, "I am safe to enjoy my life and expect good things." Learning to have fun is also very important. This sounds ridiculous, but many people do not know how to have fun. This is so sad. I am going to discuss this more in further chapters.

Learning to feel was something that I had to acquire. I had denied my feelings for so long, that at first I had a difficult time identifying what I was feeling. Due to repressing my negative feelings, I also repressed my positive feelings. As time went on, I learned to identify my feelings and to honour them. Wow, what a ride that was! Some days were good and some were not so good, but I did feel that was growth.

I have learned to make friends with all of my feelings. They are our indicators that something is wrong or things are good in our lives. If we are aware of our feelings and start identifying what they mean to us, then we take our power back. Substance users have difficulty with this, as they spent a lot of time medicating their feelings by using. I spend a great deal of time with clients assisting them in learning to identify their feelings and how to deal effectively with them.

First, it is important to realize that our feelings are not out to get us and that we have them for a reason. They are telling us something, so we need to pay attention. If we don't, then we abandon ourselves. When we actually feel our feelings, they release and we can move through them. Then we can act on what it is we need to do.

To summarize, co-dependency in essence is others centered, meeting the needs of others at our own expense, (self-abandonment). These defense mechanisms served you at some time in your life, however, now they may be causing you pain and turmoil. You can change this and create a more meaningful and happy life. You deserve to be happy and to be loved.

Trauma:
Due to the tragic death of my father, I endured trauma. This was life changing for me and I had to take the time to heal and work through my symptoms. For a while after the incident, I had a difficult time being around police. Shortly after my Dad's death, I hit a deer with my car. The next day, a police officer met with me at work to go over the paper work. It was an unexpected visit, so I was not mentally prepared. The whole time he was there, I kept looking at his gun, thinking that my Dad was shot 6 times. After he left, my supervisor happened to call me. I broke down on the phone and talked to her for a while. She encouraged me to go home and take care of myself. I went home and spent the rest of the day taking care of myself. I nurtured myself and spent time with supportive people. I used the tools I had learned as a therapist to ground myself and work through the trauma that had re-emerged in my mind. These tools were essential to my healing. I will share these strategies with you in hopes that you too can utilize these tools when necessary.

Unfortunately, in this life many of us will experience trauma. It is life changing and it is important to understand it, so you can manage the symptoms and go on living a good life, despite the devastating memories and symptoms that trauma leaves in its trail.

Examples of traumatic experiences are abuse, both sexual and physical, witnessing violence, war, witnessing death or a near death experience for yourself. Most people who I have worked with that have substance use issues, also have experienced trauma. People will use substances to medicate the pain associated with the trauma. This becomes a vicious cycle for them. I help them to manage their symptoms and explain what is happening to their body, so that they can deal with the symptoms more effectively. This then gives them some breathing room to deal with their substance abuse issues. It is also important to teach them healthy coping strategies to incorporate, so that when they experience symptoms, they have some tools to assist them. I have had the privilege of working with therapists who are well educated about trauma. Due to this, I have learned about how trauma affects the brain and bodily responses.

People who have experienced trauma that lead to Post-Traumatic Stress Disorder (PTSD) have several regions in the brain that are different from those who have healthy brain functionality. These regions are responsible for triggering symptoms of PTSD.

These regions impact stress and emotional responses. Therefore, the victim of trauma will continue to respond to stress differently. Memory functions that distinguish the difference between past and present are affected. As a result, the individual loses their ability to discriminate between time contexts correctly. Also, the ability to regulate emotional responses is decreased. This explains why individuals who experience trauma exhibit anxiety, fear and dramatic stress responses, when they experience an incident that is remotely connected to a past experience.

In some cases, an individual may react strongly to just witnessing another person who is exhibiting fear. Startle responses, flashbacks and intrusive memories can also be experienced.

It is important to note that the functionality of the brain can be reversible. The human brain is amazing with its ability to regenerate through medication and behavioural therapy.

When learning about trauma and attaining tools to manage trauma symptoms, it is vital that the person recognizes the importance of safety.

When I work with people who have experienced trauma, I talk to them about the importance of feeling safe. Safety is vital to a person's healing and their ability to incorporate strategies. Having a safe place to live and safe people for support is important. Also, creating a safe place with items that are soothing is helpful.

Learning to ground and breathe is also very effective in dealing with symptoms.

I teach clients to breathe slow and deep into their abdomen. I also incorporate soothing words, which they can tell themselves, such as, "Right now I am safe, all is well." When an individual is experiencing a flashback, it is important for them to ground themselves in the time/space/reality of the present. A flashback is a past trauma, which is replayed with great intensity. In many cases, the person may not be able to separate the flashback from present reality. The entire nervous system is triggered when experiencing a flashback. These can also occur in sleep as a nightmare or vivid dream.

I have taught clients to feel what is around them, thus orienting themselves to the year and where they are. For example, I feel the couch underneath me. It is warm and soft, it is 2016 and I am in my home. This helps to bring them back to the present. This takes practice. I advise them to work on the breathing and grounding daily, so that it comes naturally when they need to use the strategies. Also, putting your feet in the sand, grass, and water. Imagining sending roots into the earth and breathing the earth's energy is grounding. Carrying a stone, crystal or object that signifies calm, safety or strength is also very helpful. Imagining a safe place in your mind is helpful, especially if you are in a store or on a bus. Some people find relief in journaling their thoughts and feelings as well. This can be a great strategy to use in many situations. Before you go to bed, it is important to use rituals that are soothing and calming to your mind. Do not read or watch violence, as this may increase your nightmares. You can also visualize putting the flashback in a container. This way you have control of the flashback and you can put it away somewhere contained and outside of your safe space.

Find something soothing, such as reading positive books, having a bath, listening to relaxation CDs, praying, meditation, or cuddling with a teddy bear, pet, or loving partner.

Trauma is a huge topic and the information shared here is just a small portion of what is available. I hope that you can use the techniques that I have shared to your advantage and utilize them when symptoms arise. If this is not enough for you, then working with a trauma therapist may be the next step in your journey of healing. Delving into trauma without support is not a good idea, as it may cause more symptoms and further traumatize you. I refer clients to trauma specialists if they want to do trauma work.

Learning to regulate emotions and assisting with self-soothing strategies are modalities therapists use to assist with trauma symptoms.

Mental Health:
I have worked with individuals who have suffered from the effects of mental health issues for years. There are many types of mental health issues that can plague people's lives. Some of these issues are depression, anxiety, bipolar disorder, schizophrenia and personality disorders. I myself have experienced symptoms of depression and anxiety over the years. Most of the time, my symptoms of depression have been situational due to a loss in my life or a traumatic situation.

After my Dad's death, I certainly experienced symptoms of both, due to the situation I had just endured. Fortunately, I found the right assistance, via seeing a therapist and alternative measures. In a few instances, I went on medication to alleviate my symptoms. I am going to share some of the strategies I used that have helped me immensely. If you are experiencing mental health issues, it is important to seek help. The strategies that I used were in conjunction with therapy and medication. You can enjoy life again and engage back into your community. There is help and you are not alone. In my experience, when I dealt with depression, I had regrets of the past and had turned my anger inward. My co-dependency had an influence on my depression and anxiety symptoms. After I had my son, I experienced postpartum depression. At that time in my life, I had no idea what was wrong with me, but I knew that something was very wrong. I was not myself. I felt irritated, overwhelmed, sad, restless, tired, suicidal ideation and hopeless. I was not present emotionally, and I feared that my children would suffer. I sought therapy and it helped. It was at that time in my life that I decided I wanted to become a counsellor. I realized that many people had depression, and I wanted to help others like I had been helped. I talked to my therapist about it and he encouraged me to follow my heart. If you are feeling any of these symptoms, please seek help. Treatment is available, allowing you and your children to have a great life.

After I had changed some of my behaviours and thought systems, my symptoms decreased. I also would spend time in nature, the sunlight, I exercised, and I spent time with supportive people. I also did things that I loved to do. I found that my pets were extremely therapeutic. I believe that my anxiety symptoms were fear based, resulting in dread of an impending negative future. I managed my anxiety by meditation and breathing exercises, physical activity and also monitoring my thoughts. I have found that during stressful times in my life, my anxiety will increase and I have to take time to self-care. There is such a stigma around mental health and addiction, but many people experience these issues. It is so important to reach out and ask for help. Learn about mental health and ways to increase the quality of your life. There will be more information about mental health issues on our website.

Now that you have learned about some of the adversities you may experience in life, you can see the crucial need for self-care that is essential for any transformation. Go to our web site at www.themagicwithinseries.com to find more information regarding this topic on the bonuses and resources pages.

Chapter 4

Self-Care is Essential for Transforming

Self-care is essential for a healthy and thriving life. It is so important to understand how self-care can literally change your life in a positive way. As a therapist, I have to take the time to self-care daily. I have learned to take time every day to engage in healthy practices to ensure my own wellbeing and a healthy lifestyle. When working with people who are unhappy and struggling with life, it is important that I don't take home their stories and energy.

It is important to think about what you are feeding yourself. Not just food, but in everything that you do. You eat food every day, you drink, breathe, sleep, spend time with others, and watch TV, read, talk, think, and act. How are these things affecting you? What you take into your body, mind, heart and soul will affect you. It is imperative that you are mindful of what you are inviting into your body, mind and soul.

Nutrition:
This sounds so silly, but many people have no idea how to eat healthy. I find that the people I work with drink coffee, smoke tobacco and eat sugar in excess. This is not a healthy way to live. I discuss with them the need for healthy food. Nutrients are very important to the health of our bodies and mind. Eating regular nutritious meals daily is important, and the Canada food guide is a good place to start. When you feed your body nutritious food, you feel better. Pay attention to the way your body reacts to certain foods and listen to it. I am very aware of how my body reacts to certain foods. I find that when I eat food that is alive, I feel better.

Water:
Water is so important to the maintenance and hydration of the body. Many people drink coffee, tea, soda and sugary beverages, but don't think about the fact that they may be dehydrating their bodies. When the body is dehydrated, a person can experience headaches, tiredness, dizziness, light-headedness, dry mouth and constipation. When a person takes in a lot of caffeine, they will experience increased anxiety. Caffeine is a stimulant, so coffee, tea and energy drinks can increase the symptoms of anxiety.

Rest & Relaxation:
The way our society is today, many people are on the run constantly. Parents work full time jobs, go home, eat supper on the run and take their kids to an extracurricular sport or activity. Then they go home, get homework done with the kids, bath them and drop into bed, before getting up to do it all over again the next day. It is important to take time to rest and just be. People are running around exhausted in today's world. When a person takes time to be and rest, they will find that they are more at peace, more creative, able to solve problems, and just enjoy life more. Give yourself permission to have regular time outs for yourself to breathe and just BE. Doing activities, such as yoga, tai chi, reading, meditating, gardening, walking the dog, bathing, listening to relaxing music, art, getting a massage, and walking in nature, are all many ways you can take time out for yourself. You deserve to take time out regularly.

Another part of self-care is socializing. Isolating is not a healthy way to live. Taking time to be with other people and having fun is an important element of self-care. Pay attention to the people that you are spending time with. Do you feel good when you are with them? Do they inspire and uplift you? Do you feel supported? Do they tell you the truth? These are things to think about when choosing people to spend time with.

I have a motto, which is that I only spend time with supportive, loving, and caring people. If a person puts me down, belittles me, and is abusive in any way, then I cut them out of my life. I guard my energy and time with care. This is to make sure that the people and places I am spending time with are having a positive effect on me. We are energetic beings and constantly exchanging energy with each other. I want to be exchanging positive energy with people. Have you ever found that when you are with certain people you leave feeling tired, sad, and maybe irritated? You just exchanged energy with them and you ended up taking on some of their negative energy. This occurs to us all of the time. Pay attention to how you feel around other people and places. Places also have energy. Have you ever gone somewhere and felt a bad vibe? Pay attention to that also. If you go to a party or social event and the energy is low, you will feel it. You may become sleepy, irritable, frustrated, uneasy or just out of sorts. If this happens, you just walked into some energy that is not resonating with you.

Fun:

Fun is a word that many people have forgotten in today's world. They think that it is just for kids. It is imperative to have fun with self-care. Fun makes life sweeter, it gives us a reason to get up in the morning, and something to look forward to in life. I encourage my clients to allow themselves to be child-like. Do child-like things, enjoy life to the fullest. Eat ice cream and actually enjoy the taste of it. Play, go to the beach and play in the waves, make sand castles, and walk in the rain. I love spending time with my grandson. I love my play dates with him. I get down on my hands and knees and play with him. We laugh, sing, act silly, get dirty, eat ice cream, run around and enjoy our time together immensely. It is like seeing the world again for the first time. Everything is exciting, from butterflies, birds, dogs, lakes, stones, mud, rain, snow and rainbows. One day, he was at my house and it started snowing really big flakes. He saw them out the window and he was screaming with amusement. We went outside and put our hands up to the sky, watching the snowflakes come down and land on our faces and in our hair. We tried to catch them, laughing and squealing with delight. That is living in the moment and seeing snowflakes like it was the first time. I have disliked the snow for many years and I do not look forward to the winters. When I am with my grandson, however, the snow is fun. We play in it. His presence changes everything in my life, and I am so grateful for this little angel in my world. The key is to see the world through innocent eyes every day and really see the life and magic around me. I have days when I do that, especially when I am not rushing off to work or to an appointment. I have to slow down and as they say "smell the roses". Have fun and your body, mind and soul will thank you for it. Your immune system will function better, your mind will be cleared, and your heart will sing with joy. Try to be a kid for a day. Life is too short to not live it happily. Are you really living?

Kindness:
Kindness is a way to live that offers a joy that I cannot explain. Have you ever done something kind for someone and you could feel in your heart the joy of the act? Have you experienced tears of joy after helping someone? Have you ever been so happy for someone that you cried tears of joy? Extending kindness changes our energy field. It puts joy in our heart, mind and soul. Kindness also sends out a ripple effect to the universe that not only affects you, but can also affect many people or animals. Think about it. Let's say you do an act of kindness for a person, that act of kindness makes their day, they go home smiling and happy. As a result, they treat their partner in a kind way. Their partner goes to work and is kind to their co-worker,

that co-worker goes home and is kind to their child, the child goes to school and is kind to another child, that child goes home and is kind to their dog.

It could go on and on. The opposite is also true if a person is cruel to another person. The same ripple effect will occur. We don't know where our kindness will end. So be kind, and pay it forward.

If someone ever says to me, "How can I repay you?" I say pay it forward and do something kind for someone else. Kindness will also come around full swing. At some point, someone will be kind to you, because that is one of the laws of the universe. Be careful what you put out there, because it will come back to you. So chose kindness, love, appreciation and gratitude.

Gratitude:
Have an attitude of gratitude. Gratitude is another feeling that I cannot accurately explain. I was once in Florida with my whole family. We would often vacation together as a large group. I was walking alone on the beach and an intense feeling of gratitude overcame me. I was so thankful to have time with my whole family and the feeling that came over me was indescribable. I felt like I was one with the universe, like I was connected on an energetic level. My

energy was one with everything around me, including the ocean, sand, sun, wind, and birds. It felt so amazing and the only way I can describe it is bliss of the spirit. I have never felt such an intense feeling since then. I then realized the power of gratitude. Sometimes the feeling of gratitude comes over me at times, especially when I am thankful for people in my life or particular circumstances and it makes me become teary eyed. I say thank you every day to the universe for my life and the people in it. The more you are grateful, the more life will grant you good things. Saying thank you is so easy. Say it every day and watch your life change in a positive way.

Thoughts:
Our thoughts are beyond powerful. We have no idea how powerful they truly are. If you were, then you would monitor them much more carefully and guard them with care. There was a time in my life when I hated being alone, and I was very uncomfortable in my own skin and mind. I would have to turn the TV or radio on when alone, just to cover up my toxic thoughts. When alone, I would call someone on the phone or create some kind of noise, because I could not stand my thoughts. I berated myself, put myself down, and told myself I was no good and that I didn't deserve anything good in my life. It went on and on. I was my own worst enemy. I couldn't take it anymore

and I decided to face myself and change my thoughts. I forced myself to spend hours a day in silence, with no radio, TV and no other people around me. Fortunately, it was the summer, so I went to the beach with a journal, daily meditation book and a blanket. I would read a daily meditation, journal my thoughts about it and then meditate. I would listen to the waves, the birds, feel the sun on my face, feel the ground under my body, and connect with the earth. I stayed in the present and focused on my senses, only allowing myself to feel the present moment and eventually BE. By the end of the summer, I craved this time to myself, and the TV and radio irritated me. I loved being in my own skin and it became the first part of my spiritual practice. When I dwelt on negative thoughts, it felt painful. Our thoughts literally make us or break us. We can let them take us over and live a life of unhappiness and fear or we can start paying attention to them and train ourselves to think positive thoughts. I had to feed my mind with positive thoughts, which is why I read a daily meditation. Now daily, I read positive books with good messages. I feed my mind a diet of positivity. This is as important as feeding your body nutritious food. You will be thankful for learning how to do this. You will start to feel happier, more content, and peaceful.

Affirmations:
Affirmations are also very helpful to fuel your mind with positive thoughts toward yourself. Louise Hay is known for her work on affirmations and the power they have on you. There are times when I struggle with my thoughts. However, I now know how to change them and work on my self-talk. Learn to be your own best friend and stop being your own worst enemy.

Grounding with nature is paramount to a healthy life. I love nature. When I am outside, I am so connected to the life force of the universe. I crave nature and the outdoors. I have difficulty being inside during the warm months. I want to be outside to feel and sense everything, such as the birds singing, the grass beneath my feet, the flowers blooming, the sun on my face, and the wind in my hair. This is my sanctuary and my safe place. I love animals. I want to touch them, smell them, and talk to them. I love the smell of horses. I had horses for a while and it was so therapeutic going out and just brushing them, talking to them, feeding them, and shoveling manure. Sounds crazy, but yes, even that too. What kind of nature makes your heart sing? I love water, including the ocean, a river trickling, and the waves on the lake. Take time to be in nature and feel it around you. Touch a tree and feel its energy. Everything is alive. Connect with nature and be one with it. You will not regret this natural therapy and the best thing is, it is free!

Spiritual practices & pay attention to signs:
Due to this chapter focusing on self-care, I want to share how my spirituality has been a huge factor in my own self-care and essentially changed my life. We will be discussing spirituality in more detail in another chapter.

Spirituality for me is having a connection to my higher power/creator/God/universe. To me, all of these are the same being. I connect to my spirituality through prayer, meditation, nature, people, animals, kindness, performing Reiki, sharing goodness to others, yoga, exercise, belly dancing, reading, writing, aboriginal practices, and most of all, spreading love. I went on a quest for spirituality in my late 20's. I was very unhappy, depressed and anxious most of the time. I didn't know why I was so unhappy and I was searching for answers. I decided to find my own spirituality and what that meant to me. The basis of my spirituality came from learning to meditate and connecting with my spirit. As my meditation practice became more solid, I started to get answers to questions. I found solace in meditation, and most of all, a connection to my inner being and creator. My life started to become magical. I realized that the universe would answer me by sending signs; all that I had to do was pay attention.

Here are a few examples of how I followed the signs and the magic it created in my life.

I went to an AGM (Annual General Meeting) for my place of work and they had a woman there introducing belly dancing. I had always had an interest in dance, so I thought that I would try it. The class was fun and I decided to start looking for some sort of dance class to attend in the fall. Summer came and I got busy doing other things and forgot about it. One day later in the summer, I was going through my crystals and some had words written on them, such as believe, faith and more. One that I had picked up said abundance on it. The way my fingers landed on the words I read A BUN DANCE. I instantly realized that I needed to belly dance from that message. I looked up a studio close by in North Bay and signed up for my first class. I went into the class and saw the instructor. Her name was Joany. I instantly knew that this was where I was supposed to be. Not only that, but I had to become friends with her. We ended up becoming friends and I took classes with her and enjoyed belly dancing immensely. I also ended up performing and found a new love for my body as a woman. My soul loves to dance. The best part of the whole situation is that my son and Joany's daughter met, fell in love and now I have a beautiful grandson whom I love with all of my heart. All because I listened to that message from the universe.

Another time I was at the studio waiting room, passing time until my class started. I found an article in the waiting area that caught my attention. I was having some issues with my bowels and I was open to some suggestions.

There was an article on colon hydrotherapy. The man in the article had gone for a session and his colon health changed dramatically. I instantly knew that I had to explore this, so I looked up one in North Bay and ended up booking an appointment with a woman who had worked at my agency in the past named Irene. I instantly resonated with her and went for six sessions.

Prior to seeing Irene, I had been experiencing terrible pain in my abdomen. Sometimes I had to sit for up to 45 minutes before I could stand up. I have not had any pain since having the colon hydrotherapy sessions. After I met Alan, I soon realized that he too was having colon problems, as he would have abdominal pain that was worse than mine. I talked him into going to see Irene. He reluctantly went and while he was there, Irene introduced him to moringa olifera. Moringa is a natural herb that has all of the nutrients that our bodies need to be healthy. The product also had a detoxification tea that assisted with constipation. We ordered some moringa. Within a week, Alan's colon issue had changed dramatically and the pain was gone. To this day, we still take the moringa to maintain our health and detoxify our bodies on a regular basis from all of the toxins that are in our environment, water, air, and food. We rarely get sick and our minds are clear. I am so thankful that I paid attention to that article and took action.

Later, I was having some pain in my joints, my hips and knees to the point that it was affecting my dancing. I was worried that I had arthritis and did not want to give up my dancing. I decided to meditate and connect with my body. I then realized that I needed orthotics. I went to my chiropractor and he fit me for orthotics. Within three months, my pain went away and I was dancing up a storm.

I could go on and on about different things that have happened to me when I listened and paid attention. Life becomes magical when you start to trust and pay attention to the signs.

Due to these three instances, I became healthier, pain free, found a passion for dancing, made a new friend, and best of all, was blessed with an angel, my grandson! Learning to trust, listen and pay attention to what is going on around you can become a blessing in your life. I am so grateful that I have listened and trusted enough to move forward in the direction that I was shown. I hope that you will have an open mind and make self-care a priority in your life. You are worth it!

Chapter 5

Look Within: The Magic Starts Here

I have spent plenty of time in my life where I thought that when I get this job I will be happy, or when I meet the right man I will enjoy life more. I would look outside of myself for happiness in other people, places or things. Many people do this and waste the precious time of the present. Unfortunately, we look in the wrong places for answers to our own peace and happiness. People will search their whole life looking for meaning and happiness in things, such as substance use, work, car, house, retirement, partners and more. Have you ever noticed that once you get what you think will make you happy, the happiness is short lived? Then you go on to the next "thing", hoping it will be the answer. It becomes a vicious cycle that never seems to end in the happiness you crave.

The reason is because happiness is found within, not externally. When I work with clients, one of the main things that I emphasize to them is that they have the answers. They will ask me questions as if I have the answers. Maybe I have an idea that can guide them. However, I will counter with the question, "What do you think?" It is important to go within and find your answers. Many people feel lost and tell me, "I have no idea that is why I am here." My goal is to help people become independent and learn to find their peace, happiness and answers from tapping within their own wisdom. This is not something that happens overnight. It takes time and patience, but it is possible and empowering. I find that for me, I have to get quiet and listen. That means quieting my mind. Sometimes just doing something different, like going for a walk, listening to music, doing the dishes, or meditating can do the trick. All of a sudden, I get the answer.

Sometimes people have difficulty doing this because they don't trust themselves. One way to begin on your journey of learning is to connect and trust your own gut instinct. You can do this by getting quiet, taking a deep breath and asking yourself a question. It is important to ask a positive question so that your mind comes up with a positive answer. Also, the answer may not come right away. Usually with me, it will come later when I least expect it. Here is an example:

Let's say you want to make more money in your life and you are searching for a way to increase your income.

You can ask yourself, "How can I increase the income in my life in a productive way that resonates with my morals and interests?" OR you could ask yourself, "How did I ever get into this financial mess? What is wrong with me? How can I make some more money?"

See the difference? The second way sends out a negative message and the answer may not be the best one to benefit you.

We have amazing minds. The Reticular Activating System (RAS) is an amazing functional system in your brain. When you are searching for something, it will search through information and experiences to find what you are looking for. The function of the RAS is to screen and decipher what it is that is important to you. We are so bombarded by things in our environment that our conscious mind has a lot of elements to screen out. Have you ever noticed that when you buy a new car, all of a sudden you see that make of car everywhere? That is the RAS in action. We have amazing and very powerful minds. It is important to use your mind in a positive and constructive way. I often tell my clients, "You only see what you are looking for."

What is it that you are looking for? Are you noticing the beautiful things in life, such as love, laughter, sunlight, nature, animals, joy, peace, and health? Or are you noticing the pain, anger, jealousy, frustrations, lack, fear and struggle?

What you think about expands and brings you more of what you are focused on. So focus on the good, the love, and the beauty to watch your life unfold in a magnificent way all around you. Just try it for a week and see what happens. Don't complain, only say positive words, be thankful, and have an attitude of gratitude. See the world through the eyes of a child. Listen to your gut, pay attention to your body as it speaks to you. Listen to your spirit and follow your heart. Most of all, love yourself!

Happiness is a state of mind. First, you have to accept the fact that you may not have the life you want to live at this time. It does not mean that you won't find happiness. It means that only you can make yourself truly happy. True happiness takes practice and work. It is not looking at what others have or what you are missing. It is looking at what you have and feeling grateful that you have it. Do not let fear stop you from looking within. You may find out that you are capable of great things.

Alan

In 2007, I had to face my fear and virtually start over with just about nothing. All I had was determination. I had a job working out of town for CN rail that paid me $80,000 yearly to do very little. Most people would be happy with getting a lot of money to do very little. I was not happy. I felt like there was something missing in life. The ironic part was I was married and making a lot of money, but I lived from paycheck to paycheck. My marriage ended. I had put everything I had into that marriage and I just ended up being another fool.

Suddenly, I was faced with the biggest decision of my life. What was I going to do? I had my boys living with me at that time and had a job where I worked out of town. Not a good situation to raise teenage boys in. I quit that job where I had seniority, security and was about 11 years away from retiring. The job I had for 26 years was my identity and I quit to be at home to raise teenagers. This was more frightening than when I went skydiving. But this was the beginning of finding true happiness for myself. I did get a good job at home and hanging out with my kids turned out to be the greatest thing that ever happened. My daughter moved in with us as well. So there I was, a single Dad living with three teenagers. Wow, this was a big change! It was very scary, but it was also very helpful to my own recovery.

I still felt like there was something missing. A few years later, I got laid off and had to collect employment insurance. In just over two years, I had gone from making $80,000 a year to making less than $20,000. Most people would not be able to find anything good about this situation. This was the time when I found true happiness. I had very little when my marriage ended. I was actually given furniture from an ex-girlfriend whom I had children with.

One day, it came to me. I was an unemployed father raising three teenagers and barely making the payments. I finally was able to see that money does not buy you happiness. Instead, I was able to see what I truly had. I was alive. I had kids living with me and I had everything I needed to see and feel true happiness. Life was not all about trying to keep up with my neighbors. Life was not about what I did not have. Life was about what I had here and now. My relationship with my kids was one of the most powerful turning points in my life.

As my view of life changed, so did the opportunities. I went back to college at 47 years old. Yes, you read that right, 47 years old. I worked to become a Social Service Worker. What a change from being a heavy machine operator for 28 years to entering social services. I was listening to my gut tell me that this was something I wanted to do.

So back to school I went. I actually went to college with both of my boys. That was very interesting.

School taught me a lot about helping others, teaching them to empower themselves, but it also showed me some things about myself. Things I did not want to hear or like about myself.

I listened to what people were saying to me and took the steps to make the final changes I needed to make. I ended up doing my final four-month placement at an addiction rehabilitation program.

That is where I met my friend and mentor, a great program director named Kim. She taught me more about counselling people with or without addictions. It is because of her guidance and teachings that I became the counsellor I am today.

Look within yourself because the answers are there. Stop and really listen. Be honest with yourself. If you are not happy, then look at what is it that is keeping you from finding happiness.

Was any of this easy? Not really. I am only telling you these things so that you see it is possible. I am a totally different person than I was when I was growing up or in my twenties or thirties. I am just like you. I had doubts. My thoughts were, "I am nobody special, and I am not smart enough. I have been out of school for years." What I finally did was listen to what my gut was telling me. I had felt for years that there must be something more to life. That I was meant to be doing something more fulfilling. That I could do anything I wanted if I just put my heart into it. All I did was practice and practice. I learned that anything was possible. I was no one special, but I was able to become someone special. You too can change and have the life you want. Go to our website, www.themagicwithinseries.com for more helpful tips on how to create the changes you want. The next chapter is going to give you a taste of what you can do.

Chapter 6

Letting Go of Your Past

Cindy

I have spent most of my life living in the past unknowingly. My thoughts and beliefs were based on my past experiences. I would perceive my world through the lens of my past and make decisions based on past events. In some cases, it worked to my advantage, and in some cases, it resulted in creating the same situation over and over in my life.

Over the years, I have worked on my past and learned from the mistakes that I have made. This gave me the opportunity to make better decisions in my future.

Acceptance and awareness are the key and your first step to acknowledging living in the past.

I had to accept that my life was a manifestation of my thoughts, beliefs and behaviours and to completely become aware of how it impacted my life circumstances. For instance, I now realize that one way that I was living in the past was when I was on vacation. I meditate while on vacation to assist in clearing my mind and to change my thoughts to a higher vibration. While meditating, I came to a realization that I was holding onto some of my Dad's beliefs about money. Therefore, it was keeping me stuck in the past with his beliefs. I also realized that I was doing that to honour him and his death. That was a huge awakening for me, as the last thing that I wanted to do was honour his beliefs about money. He lived his life in poverty and full of fear about money issues. I quickly decided to change that thought system and my beliefs underlying money.

When I started exploring this, I then realized there were many of his beliefs that I still identified with, but they were not serving me. I wrote out as many as I could think of and then on another piece of paper wrote out the belief that I chose to believe instead. I burnt the messages that no longer served me and kept the ones that now served me. I also realized that my Dad would not want me to keep beliefs that are not self-serving to honour him. I know that he would want me to be happy. To honour him, I made positive changes. In order to come to this awareness, I had to have an open mind. This allowed me to become aware of my thought patterns and beliefs. I then had to have the willingness to make the changes and be completely open to accepting the reality that I was living in. Many times, we live in denial and this leaves us no room to grow and change. Therefore, becoming aware is the first step, and then taking positive action can change your life.

I also had to realize that my past had created my present situation. I had made decisions in the past that led to my present situation. I also held beliefs in the past that led to my present situation. I realized that I had to let go of those beliefs that did not serve me any longer.

This can also occur when you hold resentments from the past. When a person holds resentments, it is like having an energetic cord attached to the person that you have resentment toward. Instead of making positive changes in the future, you end up manifesting a very similar situation to the one you are so disgusted with.

Let's use the example of a separation. You leave a partner for whatever reason or your partner leaves you. You start dating again and say, "I am never going to put up with that again". You meet someone and it seems great. Down the road, however, you find yourself in a similar situation or worse. You think, "How did this happen to me again?" This is an example of how your past can bite you in the butt. It is important to address the issues that you dealt with in your prior relationship and to let go of the resentments in order to move forward without drawing that energy into your next relationship.

Past pain, anger, resentments, and grief that is not resolved will stay attached to you and follow you wherever you go. It is like you have chains attached to you and the past is attached to the chains like big boulders. No wonder people feel exhausted and sick when they carry their past around with them for years, or in some cases, the rest of their lives. When I do work on breaking free from my past, I do an energetic meditation. I imagine the person that I have issues with and see an energetic cord attached from myself to that other person. I see my energy leaking from me to them. I see how this is depleting my energy system and how it is not serving me any longer. I decide that I no longer want to allow this to deplete my precious energy system, so I decide to cut that cord. I imagine having a big sword and I cut the cord from every angle of my body. Pay attention to where you see the cord. Is it attached to your abdomen, chest, back, or head? Think about your body and if you are having any physical issues in that area. I cut the cords and then imagine that I have a vacuum that sucks up any excess negative energy. I then fill myself with light to protect me and keep me in a positive space. Symbolic work like this can be very powerful for many issues that you want to release. You can be creative with this and do it in a way that resonates with you. If you continue to carry these attachments, you will end up being a prisoner to your own past and you will continue to make the same decisions over and over in your life. You may have to do this many times. Every time you think about that person or situation in a negative way, you will create that negative energy again.

Letting go with love and forgiveness of yourself and others:
The next step is letting go with love and forgiveness. Holding onto resentments only hurts the person holding the resentment. Forgiveness is for your healing and it is not condoning the behaviour of the other person. This is a very powerful tool. Forgiveness can change your life for the better. It sets you free of the past, along with the pain and suffering attached to it. I was in disbelief when the deceased officer's widow asked everyone at his funeral to forgive my Dad! She is a very wise woman. That early in her grief, she realized the importance of forgiveness. She truly is an amazing woman who demonstrated strength

and forgiveness herself. Forgiveness is not easy and sometimes it is a process. I link it to the stages of grief. Sometimes we need to go through the process of loss and allow ourselves to release the feelings associated with that loss, before we can forgive. Many times I thought that I had forgiven someone and then it popped up again. I thought I had worked through that, but I had to do the work again. I have to honour where I am in my healing process and work with the feelings that are being presented.

In time I will forgive, but it just may not be right now. For some reason, I am not ready. However, I know that in time I will continue to move forward as long as I am open to doing the work involved, which includes uncomfortable feelings at times.

Forgiving myself is also something that I have to keep in mind, as many times the resentment I hold is towards myself. Having love, understanding and compassion is key to this process.

Realizing that you did the best you could in that situation and that you cannot go back and change the situation helps in the process. However, you can change the future by letting go and forgiving yourself. As I said earlier, my motto is, "Do I want to become bitter or better?" I choose BETTER. What do you choose?

In the next chapter, we are going to discuss how your beliefs and programming can affect your life. Once you become aware of your programming, explore your beliefs and change these beliefs, you can make positive changes in your future!

Alan

My partner is right in her advice on letting go, but being a guy, I know how hard it is to let go of something or someone that you feel has wronged you. I struggled to let go of things in my past for years. I was very angry with someone who had sexually abused me when I was around ten years old. I never told anyone, especially my parents. Firstly, I did not think they would believe it happened. I even went as far as blaming myself for what happened, saying that I deserved to be punished. I will talk more about this incident in a later chapter.

I really think my ego was in the way of my healing. At first, it was disbelieving the incident had ever happened. But after a few years, the disbelieving became anger that was like a raging fire. There came a day in my twenties when one of my best friends told me that I was really scary when I got mad. I was actually really hurt when he said this to me. Of course, I never showed that emotion. Instead, I justified my actions.

Then I remember being all alone and making excuses for my actions. I even blamed others for what I was doing. As I sat there virtually in tears and shaking, I realized I was now angry with myself for becoming something I did not like or want to be. I had to take a long hard look at who I was. As I sat there, I started to remember something from my past. Something I tried really hard to bury. I was still angry with myself for that incident that happened nearly 16 years earlier.

That was the day I realized I was holding on to someone else's beliefs. The day I was assaulted when I was a kid, that person said to me that, I deserved to be punished for what I had done. I will explain it all in a later chapter.

I had to start by forgiving myself. Yes, I had to forgive myself for what someone else did. As a kid, I blamed myself for what happened to me. I even made myself believe I deserved what had happened. This is where my true anger was.

At this time in my life, I started to understand and see things clearer. I was holding onto something that had caused me so much pain that I tried my best to bury it. I had never ever told anyone else. Something from 16 years ago was still affecting me in my late twenties.

The first step to letting go of my anger was to not blame myself for what had happened so long ago. I recognized that I was a victim of a very sick man. I told myself many times over the next few months that it was not my fault. I told myself this so many times that I began to believe it. I had to change more than just that. I had to tell myself that it was not worth being mad anymore. It took practice and patience, but I was able to start the healing process. This was big for me, and as time went on, I even began to like myself again.

I was one of those guys. You know them as very tough, never needs help, and never shows weakness. I was all of those things and much more. All of these beliefs were from my father and my peer group, such as the friends I hung out with and fellow students from school. But I also created beliefs from the shows I watched and the movies I went to see. So when I talked about forgiveness and letting go, let me tell you that was really hard for a guy like me, but I did succeed in doing just that.

Letting go of your past is one of the most important things you will need to do. As a counsellor, I asked my clients what would happen if they drove their cars forward, but would only look into their rear view mirrors. Almost all said they would crash. Well that is what living in the past will do to your life. It will cause you to crash and not have the life you want.

Go to our web site www.themagicwithinseries.com and we will share with you various strategies for letting go and creating the future you are truly looking for. The next chapter is the first step in retraining your beliefs and changing your future.

Chapter 7

Reprogram Your Mind and Release Your Inner Power

Reprogramming your mind is a huge and powerful way to change your life. This takes courage, as well as complete awareness to explore your beliefs, patience and work.

> *It is not the events of our lives that shape us,*
> *But the belief as to what those events mean.*
> *-Tony Robbins*

In order to do this, you have to become aware of and start challenging your beliefs. Do you ever wonder why you end up in the same situation over and over? Do you ask yourself how you got there again? This happens because of your ingrained subconscious belief systems, which are deeply entrenched. Often times, we don't even know what our beliefs are until something happens that gives us an "aha" moment. The lights come on and we are "enlightened" about that particular belief. The irony here is that our beliefs are paramount in setting the direction of our lives and experiences.

So it is very important that we understand our belief systems. Our minds are so very powerful. Many of us have no idea of the power that we have within us that drives much of our lives.

Our beliefs can literally save our lives or cause turmoil. For instance, many of us are familiar with the placebo effect. This is amazing proof of the power of our beliefs. People will be given a sugar pill without being aware that it is a placebo. They are told that this pill will make them better and voila, they get better. It was not the pill the made them better. It was their belief that it would make them better. So how do we identify our beliefs and change them to create positive results in our lives?

It is so important in the helping field to instill hope in people. Many times if a person is told that there is hope then they will start to improve, but only if they believe the statement.

Beliefs can originate from perceptions that we have attached to an experience. A belief is created when we become certain about something that we have experienced.

Often our beliefs are not accurate and they can sometimes be irrational, such as when we are children and we see the world through a child's mind. We may also take on other people's beliefs that don't serve us. However, we are not always aware that we have even done so, such as my experience of taking on my Dad's beliefs about money. These beliefs become ingrained in our mind and we will act on them throughout our lives.

Our beliefs are like a reflection in the mirror. What do you see? One way to become aware of your beliefs is to look at your life.

Your experiences will reflect your beliefs.

For example, maybe you don't have many very close friends. You find that most of your friends are superficial and they are not deep and caring individuals. This experience could be a result of believing that when people get to know you, they will dislike you. Even when someone does like you, you will sabotage the relationship because of your belief.

You will do this by creating something that will end or damage the relationship to keep the status quo of a "superficial relationship".

Self-prophesying beliefs are that strong!

Have you heard of the saying, "You only see what you look for?" You could think of it as, "All of us wear glasses." My glasses are different then your glasses. I may perceive a situation totally differently than you would due to the glasses that I wear. That is because of our different beliefs and perceptions in life. Upon examination of your life, you can identify what beliefs are keeping you from living the life that you want, and what beliefs are working for you.

The origins of our beliefs come from our childhood. When we are born, we are like a blank piece of paper. We had no beliefs or thoughts about life. Someone started to write on your precious blank page. They started writing things, such as, you are an idiot, how can you be so stupid, you should be ashamed of yourself, you will never amount to anything. Or they could be positive thoughts, such as you are amazing and beautiful, you are very smart, you can do whatever you set your mind to do, and you are a creator with the ability to create the life of your dreams.

Can you relate to any of these statements? When you are a child, you are like a sponge and you will soak up beliefs without even knowing it. A child will pick up ideas and make sense of them in their tiny brain by building a belief system that may not be an accurate depiction of what is going on around them. It is the perception that creates the belief. An example would be, a young boy witnesses his father physically abusing his mother. One perception and belief he may file in his mind would be, women need to be beaten, or he may file away a belief that I will never treat a woman like that and when I get older I will protect women. It is the perception that forms the belief. Children from the same family can grow up and have totally different belief systems.

Do you have relationship problems, money problems, overweight issues, and health issues? The evidence of your life will demonstrate your beliefs. Beliefs can be hidden underneath your thoughts. In cognitive therapy, a therapist will help you to examine the automatic thoughts that you think all day long. If you go deeper, then you can tap into the beliefs that are driving those thoughts.

Here is an example of how you can tap into your belief systems around life. It is vitally important for you to be brutally honest in order to explore your belief systems.

What do you think about life in general?

Write down some of your thoughts/ beliefs about life.

Example: A belief that I used to carry was: Life is very hard, be very afraid.

No wonder I spent years living with anxiety and being depressed. I was afraid to live due to this destructive belief. I also realized that this belief came from my Dad, as he would always talk about how difficult life was and he demonstrated his fear of life.

I took this belief on and wore it into my adult years. I have now decided to believe instead that, "All is well." Life is a journey of exciting adventures awaiting me, and I can handle whatever comes my way. I now have faith in myself and in the universe to support me in my endeavors.

I feel much better and I now live life, looking forward to my next adventure.

Write down the issues that you are facing in your life.

Ask yourself:
What are my thoughts/beliefs about these issues?
Where did they come from?
How strong are they?
Are they rational?

Can I dispute this belief; or is there evidence of this belief? Is there evidence of an opposing belief that is more self-serving?
What are some alternative beliefs that will serve me in my life now?

Continue writing until you have no more to say.

Read the self-defeating beliefs, talk about them, and decide to let them go. Write down the opposite of that belief, creating one that serves you, and then burn the ones you don't want. Decide that these beliefs will no longer sabotage your life. Then take the new beliefs and create affirmations out of them.

Ex: I am a strong and capable person; I can create the life of my dreams. I am abundant and I am living a life of abundance.

Even though this is not present in your reality yet, keep reading them and everyday imagine the new life that you want.

I wanted to find a good partner, who is loving, generous, kind, gentle, handsome, fun, and adventurous. I made a booklet, took pictures from magazines and wrote my book on my new amazing relationship. I put in pictures of what my new partner would be like and our relationship.

Twice a day, I would look at my book and I imagined what my life would be like with this amazing relationship. Within four months, I met Alan. Ironically, he had all of the qualities that I had in my book. Coincidence? I don't think so. That was the power of my mind and the universe manifesting to me what I had put out there!

Also, prior to doing this, I had to work on my belief that I deserved to have a wonderful relationship. If I did not believe that I deserved a healthy and wonderful relationship, then I would not have created it in my life.

Feeling unworthy and undeserving is a huge issue for many people on the path to be able to create the life that they want.

Make sure that you explore this in order to change your life for the better. If you do not, then the work on money, relationships or other goals will not be effective. This is because you are sabotaging your efforts with a self-defeating belief of "I am not worthy". To find more information on self-prophecy, go to our web site at www.themagicwithinseries.com.

What is your message?

What message are you sending to others? Think about it. I have had clients say to me, "I feel like I have a sign on my forehead saying, "Take advantage of me". They are sending that message to others. It is just not on their forehead, but in their energetic communication.

Other people may not see a sign, but they respond to the energy or behaviours the person demonstrates. We are all communicating to each other on a vibrational and non-verbal basis all of the time. Take a moment and ask yourself, "What message am I wearing on my forehead?"

What is my message? Your message is a collection of behaviours, body language, words that you chose to use, the tone and way you speak to people. For example, if a woman flirts with men by sending them nonverbal signals and making comments that appear flirty, then the male may think that she is coming on to him. He will then proceed to make a move toward her and think she is interested in him. However, the woman has no interest in him, as that is her usual way of communicating with men. She then wonders why men always get the wrong message from her. She is wearing a signature that is telling men that she is interested in them without knowing it.

Some people you meet and afterwards, you walk away thinking that person is arrogant, stupid, narcissistic, self-absorbed, cruel, kind, gentle, caring, hostile, or aggressive. It is important to know what your message is and if it is working for you. Maybe you wear a signature of arrogance. However, it is just a defense mechanism, when really you have low self-esteem and it is just a smoke screen. Maybe you wear a sign that you are unaware of, which is obvious to other people. If you are not sure of what your sign is, ask other people that are close to you. Also, think about how other people treat you and things that happen to you often. That maybe a clue to the signature that you wear.

As I said before, you are very powerful! Asking yourself these questions is important so that you are more aware of what circumstances you are attracting into your life.

If you can change your reflection, then your life will change. Many people are afraid of change. They will resist change and do anything possible to keep their life the same. Unfortunately trying to control this is a waste of energy, as change is inevitable. Change will happen whether you like it or not, so you might as well have some positive change occur and point your life in a more positive direction.

Yes, change is scary, but only until you face your fears and start to really get in touch with your beliefs and see where they came from. Until then, you will only get what you always got in life. We have helpful tips and real plans for assisting you to change the way you look at life. We can also provide you with personal support to help you with looking at where your beliefs come from and how to change them. All of this is on our website www.themagicwithinseries.com.

Embracing your new beliefs and taking charge of your life: We are constantly creating new beliefs. In every situation, we are deciding how to decode and store away the event in our mind. Our perceptions are based on our beliefs, so each event will be viewed through the lens of past experiences. It is important to become aware of how you perceive your life and the outcome of those perceptions. If you have a positive mindset, then your beliefs will most likely be positive. If you have a negative mindset, then your beliefs will most likely become negative. You have to pay attention to how you respond to situations, and how you feel.

Your feelings are an indicator of your thoughts and beliefs.

If you are feeling sad, resentful, angry, or frustrated most of the time, then you may want to challenge your attitude and decide if you want to live like this any longer. You have the power to decide. It is worth the effort, because you are worth the effort. With a little bit of work, you can start to make the changes you want.

What is the worst thing that could happen? There are only two answers to this question.
1) Nothing will change.
2) Everything may change and you may actually get what you have been dreaming or hoping for.

Wait till you read what we have in store for you in the next chapter.

Chapter 8

Embracing Spiritual Practices

In my life journey, I have found that my spiritual practices have been the anchor that kept me able to continue moving forward, despite sometimes overwhelming and difficult circumstances. I believe spirituality has been literally my savior during times when I felt like giving up. Surrendering to the universe was a critical, and unfortunately, last step for me. If I had surrendered sooner, I may have not suffered as much. However, I believe that what happened occurred for my growth and necessary change.

What is spirituality?
This is a question asked by many people. I guess my answer to that question is another question.

What is spirituality to you?
Spirituality is a personal thing. It is not something that everyone experiences in the same way. For me, it has not

only been a connection to my higher power but also the realization that the higher power also resides in me. I have disconnected from this power at different times in my life. I realize that when I did so, my life was much more difficult. Once I embraced my own life force, which was always flowing through me and available to me, my life became very beautiful and magical. Hence, the name of this book. I found this quote and it completely explains what my spiritually has become and how I now have evolved and exist in the universe.

"The universe is me, and I am the universe. The universe exists in me, and I exist in the universe. Light exists in me, and I exist in the light."
Mikao Usis, quoted by Hiroshi Doi in lysahino Gendai Reiki-ho

 It is important that you find what resonates with you at this time in your life. I say that because I have practiced different forms of spirituality at different times in my life depending on what was occurring. Sometimes I resonated more with a different practice and so I would use that practice.

There are different types of spiritual practices. I will touch on some here to describe how they helped me and to assist you in deciding if it is a fit for you. There is no right or wrong way to tap into your personal spirituality. It is your way and what resonates in your heart, mind and soul.

Meditation:
There are different types of meditative practices, such as mindfulness meditation, guided meditation, quieting the mind. Yoga can be a form of meditation, walking, or just being. Meditation can be as personal as spirituality.

I have practiced different types of meditation and depending on my mood, I will choose a different style. I always listen to my body and spirit, doing what I am led to do.

First of all, I encourage you to make friends with your mind, body and spirit. That may sound strange but so many of us are not at all connected to our bodies, mind and spirit. Most of the time we only live in our minds. We have no idea what our bodies and spirit are wanting or needing. I have learned to get still and listen to the quiet whispers of my body and spirit.

Sometimes we may not want to hear what is being said. Due to having a busy lifestyle, we might know that our body needs a break, but we push ourselves anyway. I find that when I do this, I end up getting sick and my body says to me, "I told you, but you didn't listen, so I slowed you down so you can rest."

I have now learned to listen and obey my body's signals. Otherwise I suffer the consequences of an illness that comes at the worst time. I find that if I check in daily with my body and listen to it, then I will know what it needs, such as exercise, water, sleep, meditation time, a friend, love, and nurturing.

It is also important to send positive messages to your body. Masaru Emoto did studies on this with water. He would take water and put words on it, such as love, gratitude, hate, and anger. He would then freeze the water and it would turn into crystals. The results were astounding, the crystals that had positive messages were beautiful and the ones with negative words were ugly. Our bodies are 70% water. When I say that your body is listening, it is listening!

If you are saying to your body phrases like you are so fat and ugly, you disgust me, and I hate you, then how do you think that your body is going to respond? Try this and see how it feels. Allow yourself to feel your body's response.

Have a bath or shower and afterwards put on a nice lotion all over your body. Start at your feet and say to them, thank you for taking me places in life, I really love you for this, you move so eloquently and I am sending you love and appreciation. Then work up your body using loving and appreciative messages all the way to your head. Continue telling your body how beautiful it is and how much you love it. Even though you may not be happy with the size of your stomach or butt, think of the good things about them. I find when I do this I can feel by body responding with love and it wants to do more for me. It also responds with a thank you for noticing and I feel like crying, as my body finally feels acknowledged for how it supports me in life. We only have one body and it has to get us through our lifetime. It is important to become friends with our body and love it, so that it can keep us healthy to do the things that we love and spend time with our loved ones to the fullest extent possible. I remember a time when I was not happy with my weight. However, I chose to tell my body that I loved it and that it was beautiful. I felt inclined to dance and watch how my body would move so eloquently. The more I watched, the more beautiful I looked in the mirror. As time went on, I ended up losing weight and my body became tighter and leaner. My feminine features shone with pride and I truly felt beautiful as a woman. It all started by acknowledging and loving myself where I was. I loved my body into a beautiful masterpiece.

Connecting to Your Spirit:

In my experience in order to connect to my spirit, I have to quiet my mind. This can be difficult at first for many people. It took me quite a while to be able to make this happen. When talking to groups of people about meditation I ask them, how would it feel for you if you had a moment of freedom from your mind and thinking? They would all say to me, "That would be such a relief, please show me how to do it!" The problem is that it takes time and practice to learn to do this. Our society has become habituated to having everything now, with immediate gratification. However, some things take time to learn and taking the time to learn how to meditate is worth it. I believe that I learned to meditate the hard way. I would lay in my tub with warm water in it and count down backwards from 20 in my head. When another thought came into my mind, I had to start over. Once I got to zero, I would then sit in silence from my thoughts. This took me a month to learn, but I was so desperate for peace that I forced myself to do it. I had to imagine a clock in a hockey area counting backward, at zero I would hear the buzzing sound and then have silence. Talk about a difficult way to learn to meditate. I did it though and it was my means of meditating for years. When I had a problem, I would meditate. In most cases, I would get the answer. Sometimes the answer would be subtle and sometimes it would be very strong. When it was strong, I would have to get up and immediately follow up with the solution, which always ended up with the outcome I was hoping for.

As time moved on, I began to do guided meditations. Guided meditations are a wonderful way to learn to meditate. You can find different types of guided meditations that will deal with many topics. I studied angels, spirit guides, energy work, light work and many more practices that enhanced my life. I shared these with my family and friends. We would all join together to share and assist each other in our spiritual growth. As you explore spirituality, you will meet likeminded people with whom you can share and enjoy their company.

Native Spirituality:
I was lucky to have close people in my life who were aboriginal, so I partook in some of the beautiful practices of the aboriginal culture. Many people are drawn to the spiritual practices of this culture, even though they have

no aboriginal ancestry. I describe these practices as sacred and they are meant to be practiced with respect and honour.

When I first heard the drumming, it spoke to my spirit to the point that it made me cry. I felt like my heart was touched. I cannot explain the feeling except that I wanted to experience more. I smudge regularly, especially when I feel that I need to cleanse my energy, my house, objects or surroundings to initiate a healing. Smudging is a ceremony that uses sacred herbs. Sage, cedar and sweet grass are the most commonly used. Sage is to cleanse negative energy, cedar is to assist in our prayers reaching the creator, and sweet grass brings in the positive spirits. The aboriginal culture believes that everything has a spirit and they have a deep respect for nature, land, animals, and people, which all have a spiritual essence. They also believe that a spirit will leave through the western doorway and return to the circle of life in the spirit world. If you would like to experience more of the aboriginal culture, you can attend a Pow Wow and hear the drumming, watch the dancing ceremonies and witness the beauty of the regalia. Here is an example of some of the beautiful teachings of the first nation people. If the world followed these teachings, it would be a much better place to live in.

The First Nation people have many teachings. These teachings have been passed down from generation to generation. There are so many teachings that many books could be written about them.

I like the Seven Grandfather teachings. They resonate with what we are trying to do with this book. The Seven Grandfather teachings are a set of teachings based on human conduct towards others.

WISDOM: To cherish knowledge is to know wisdom. Wisdom is given by the creator to be used for the good of the people.

LOVE: To know love is to know peace. Love must be unconditional. When people are weak, they need love the most.

RESPECT: To honour all of creation is to have respect. All of creation should be treated with respect. You must give respect if you wish to be respected.

BRAVERY: Bravery is to face the foe with integrity. To do what is right even when the consequences are unpleasant.

HONESTY: Honesty in facing a situation is to be brave. Always be honest in word and action. Be honest first with yourself, and it will be easier to be honest with others.

HUMILITY: Humility is to know yourself as a sacred part of creation. You are equal to others, but you are not better.

TRUTH: Truth is to know all of these things. Speak the truth. Do not deceive yourself or others.

These seven teachings stand out. There is only one race on this earth and that is the human race. We are all interconnected in one-way or another. First Nations believe that the spirits of our ancestors are with us to help and guide us on our journey through life.

12 Step Programs:
When I was training as an addiction counsellor, I had to do a co-op placement. I was lucky and I got to do my co-op at a residential treatment center. I was told to attend groups and to just observe what was going on and listen. I attended my first group and I was blown away by the spirituality of the 12-step program. I walked out of the room after group knowing deep in my heart that this was where I was supposed to be on my journey of learning spirituality. They spoke of a God that was foreign to me.

The God that I was told about was punishing, jealous, and would make me pay for my sins. The God that they talked about was loving, gentle, forgiving, and supportive. Wow, I felt like I was finally where I was supposed to be. I had been led to this type of training to further my own spiritual path. As part of my training, I had to do the first 5 steps of the AA program. I was eager to do this as I had a thirst for spiritual growth. After completing the 5th step, I went to the chapel, where I meditated and cried. I was grateful for this experience, as it propelled me forward to my next adventure and discovery of myself. I would encourage anyone to work these steps even if you do not have an addiction. I believe that you will be able to connect with the material in some way, whether it is an addiction to people, sugar, eating, work, exercise, shopping, sex, and busy- ness. We can all relate to some form of coping mechanism that can be addictive. You just change the focus from alcohol to whatever your issue is in your life.

Yoga:
Namaste: "The light in me greets the light in you."
Namaste is a greeting that people in the yoga world use when greeting one another. What a beautiful way to greet a person in our life. If we could actually see the beauty in others in this way, our relationships would heal and conflict would decrease.

Another way a person can connect spirituality is to use different practices that are experienced through the physical body. I took yoga for a while with a good friend. The experience was incredible. The whole time we did yoga my mind continued to quiet down to the point where I felt like I could just stay in a certain pose for an extended amount of time. It was almost like time stood still during that yoga class.

Then at the end we would mediate on our mats and my whole being just rested. What a glorious experience and what a great way to tap into spirituality. There are many types of yoga, so you can find one that resonates with your needs and desires.

Energy work:
As part of my spiritual journey, I wanted to learn more about energy work. I felt at my core that I was a healer and working as a therapist, I could help people. Still, I was limited as to how I could assist people.

I believe that integrating the whole individual via body, mind, and spirit and focusing on balancing the energy of the total person is essential to healing.

We are always sending and receiving energy with each other. We are energy/spiritual beings. We transmit energy signals that flow out to the universe. Our energy can be felt by other people and animals, even though they may not be aware of it. Have you even walked into a room and felt uncomfortable vibes? You then find out later that the people in the room were having a heated disagreement. That is how we are affected by the energy around us. It is very important to pay attention to this energy, as it is like your 6th sense. This 6th sense is accurate, but unfortunately, many times we dismiss these messages and sometimes end up regretting it.

You may also find that when you are around certain people, you may be left feeling drained, irritable or just out of sorts. You were just affected by the energy that person was emitting. This can also happen in places, such as homes, hotels, or any type of building. Everything has an energy frequency. Some frequencies are high and some are low. Our frequency will change depending on our mood, the thoughts we think and the words we speak. I have found that if I have been around a lower vibration, it helps if I ground myself afterwards through smudging, imagining a bubble of white light around me of protection and thinking positive thoughts. Everything has an emitting energy including music, crystals and objects. I surround myself with positive energy and people as often as possible.

I was interested in learning how help people heal through energy work. Therefore, I studied Reiki, which assists in replenishing our energy system, while it strengthens and balances our immune system. The hands of the Reiki practitioner are a conduit that the energy flows through into the receiver. As a result, no personal energy is drained from the giver. The thing that resonated for me with Reiki is that it is a loving intentional way of assisting a person in their healing process. Energy healing assists the individual in becoming connected with their soul/spirit. If the body, mind and spirit are not connected, then there cannot be complete healing. Illness will manifest itself in the physical body if the soul is not healthy. Reiki is a gentle loving healing modality that can leave a person feeling rested and rejuvenated. There are many types of energy healing modalities. Find one that resonates with your soul if you are interested in this type of healing.

"The cure of the part should not be attempted without treatment of the whole. No attempt should be made to cure the body without also curing the soul. This is the error of our day, that physicians first separate the soul from the body."
- Greek Philosopher Plato, 427-347 BC

The Law of Attraction:
The law of attraction is a very powerful law of the universe. We are vibrational beings and our thoughts vibrate and radiate a signal, which will attract a matching signal back to us like a magnet. We attract to us what we put out to the universe. We draw to us that of a similar vibration. This is why it is imperative that we pay attention to our thoughts, because they can literally cause a living hell or a life of positive experiences. When you are not in a good mood and you start your day in a negative mindset, you will notice that your day may continue to move forward in a difficult fashion. This is the law of attraction working, whether you are in favour of it or not.

When you think about a situation, then you are inviting it into your experience. A way that I found helpful to assist in creating the experience that I want is to imagine myself living my life the way I would like it to be. When I wanted to manifest a relationship, I created a book with pictures and words describing the relationship that I desired. I also imagined how wonderful it would feel to further create a powerful attraction. As I shared earlier, I met Alan within four months.

If you desire something and predominately think about the absence of it in your life, then you will create the opposite of what you want, the absence of it! The vibration that you send out is the opposite of the vibration that you are wanting. We get the essence of our thoughts, regardless if they are what we want or not. Therefore, it is important to only think about what you want. This is much easier said than done. As humans, sometimes we get caught up in the daily issues of our lives. I have found that I can become more aware of my feelings than my thoughts. I am very aware of when I am not feeling positive emotionally. I know that my thoughts create my feelings; so being aware of my feelings is a useful tool. I have some days that I am just not in a good mood. Sometimes this happens for no reason. I get up on the wrong side of the bed. On these days, I do more self-care and get more rest. Usually a bad mood for me is a lack of sleep or some stress related issue that I need to deal with. I will also do things that help my mood, such as putting on music, dancing, singing, or spending time with my grandson. His sweet innocent smile and gracious love warms my heart and I soon forget that I was not in a good mood. Sometimes when I catch myself in a bad mood, I ask myself what am I thinking about right now? If my thoughts are negative, then I intentionally think more positive thoughts. The fact is that the law of attraction is working all of the time. If you want your life to work for you, then learn more about this and pay attention to the thoughts that you are putting out, the mood you are in, and basically your attitude about life.

I also wrote earlier about how we are affected by the people that we are around, the environment we are in, the media that we watch, and the books we read. Now understanding this and how the law of attraction works, it is essential that you monitor not only the stimulation of your thoughts but the people and environment that you subject yourself to! If you constantly surrounded by violence, such as violent people, violent TV programs, violent books, and violent discussions, then it becomes normal in your life.

A way of identifying if you are in an energetic match to what you want to create is how you are feeling about it. If you are excited and happy about your life and what you are manifesting, then you will know that you are in alignment with the intention of your creation. If you are unhappy, sad and frustrated, then you are not in alignment with what you are trying to create.

To summarize, you are a magnet, and what you focus on expands. Your thoughts will create your feelings.

If you are feeling negative emotions, then you know that you are not attracting what you want. Pay attention lovingly to your feelings. Use this information to help you move forward by thinking about how you can change the attraction to what you desire. You can control this by creating a positive environment with supportive people, and being careful about what you put into your mind via TV, books, and radio. Be careful what you put into your precious body in terms of food, drink and other substances. What are you feeding yourself is a good question to ask regularly, not just food but thoughts, people, television, reading materials, and more. You are important, so decide that you are worthy of living the life of your dreams and take action.

There is a lot of literature and education that you can tap into in regard to the law of attraction.
Enjoy your journey learning about the spiritual universe, as it is a fascinating topic.

Living in the Moment:
I find that when I live in the moment, I feel vitally alive and free. I have to focus on this intently, as I can get distracted easily.

I have found that when on vacation my mind will sometimes wander to my life at home, and that is not where I want my mind to be. Therefore, I need to intentionally focus on my senses. I will feel the sun on my face, the sand beneath my feet, and the water lapping. I listen to the waves, the birds, and smell the aroma of the ocean. When eating, I have to slow down and pay attention to the texture and taste of the food. When I do this, everything slows down and I truly see the beauty of the world around me. I am actually there in that precious moment. Another way I have found to be in the moment is to learn something new. When we learn a new skill, our minds have to actually be in the moment to acquire the new task.

Have you ever thought about what you contemplate most of the time? If you really examine this, you will most likely realize that your mind is caught up in time, past or future. We are usually planning something, stressing about something coming up, or regretting the past. I was shocked when I actually considered this concept. I have found that the thing that I love the best about meditating is that I get a break from my mind constantly chattering to me. This sounds silly, but my mind is busy most of the time. I also have realized that my mind can be my own worst enemy, creating unnecessary suffering. I have learned that with meditation I can actually control my mind chatter. What a relief! I liken my mind to my ego. It is attached to things, material things, things that I have achieved, who I think that I am in regard to my career, and more. Have you ever noticed that when you meet a new person, one of the first things they ask you are, "What do you do?" It is like it is our identity. We attach ourselves to our career. What else do we attach ourselves to? The unfortunate thing is that if we don't amount to much financially, materially or career wise, we think that we are losers or worse. We appear to live in a society where that is how we identify ourselves. This is so sad. We don't need to have things to be okay. We are okay just being who we are. To add to this idea, most of us don't even know who we are. I actually do an exercise with groups that I work with. I ask them to present to the group, "Who are you?" Most people have difficulty with this and they struggle with answering the question. Do you know who you are without your stuff?

From going within and connecting with my real essence, I have tapped into who I really am and it has nothing to do with the stuff that I have. It has to do with who I am inside, my inner being. That part of me does not have to do anything to be worthy or deserving of goodness.

That part of me is all good, all perfect and completely full of love. I once experienced that part of myself in a state of meditation. The feeling was so lovely that words cannot express adequately the experience. The only way that I can express it is that it was blissful. I felt completely at peace, ageless, timeless, and full of life, radiant, expansive, luminous, weightless, full of energy, and joyful. Since then, I have realized that is who I truly am.

I realized that my mind/ego is the way I block out this experience. My spirit is my true being. Tapping into this has been transformational for me. I hope that you can find this bliss as well through whatever means works for you. This is the magic that I speak about. This is who we all are. We are beautiful, incredible beings. We are all spirits having a human experience.

The next chapter is about real life people who have overcome life adversities, how they changed their lives in positive ways, and what they are doing now. This inspires hope and shows that we all can tap into our own inner magic and enjoy an amazing life.

Chapter 9

Success Stories of Hope

Never give up
When life is a challenge
Remember it is only temporary
It is just a bend in the road
Not the end of the road.
-Tina Pauls

Tina Pauls

Tina is a very dear friend of ours. She always makes us laugh and she loves to enjoy life. Tina is helpful and generous with her staff, customers and friends. Tina is a joy to have in our life and we are very grateful to be able to call her our friend.

Tina described her life as a youngster as living a privileged life. She grew up in a wonderful family and she went into her adult years with excitement and enthusiasm.

Tina fell in love and got married. In time, her excitement turned into anxiety and fear as her husband became ill with mental health and addiction issues. He would call the police when Tina was home late from work out of concern for her safety. His behaviours became more frightening as time went on and Tina's life became a tyranny of uncertainty and doubt. He would speak in different languages during the night and she woke up numerous times, as he was choking her in her sleep.

She couldn't deal with the stress anymore, so she decided to leave. During that time, her partner went off of his medication and went missing for three months. She finally found him and informed him that their relationship was over.

So, he came back to collect his stuff from their house. While he was there he called Tina and told her that he felt old, ugly, and he did not want to live any more. He also instructed her to enter the house through the front, not the back. She then knew that something was wrong.

When Tina went home, she found him dead. He had killed himself. He left his wedding ring on the dining room table with a note. Tina called 911 and went into shock.

Still to this day, Tina suffers from PTSD symptoms. At the time, her sister found her a Christian counsellor who helped her immensely. Her counsellor met with her for three days per week for a year. Tina disclosed that it was her daughter who really pulled her out of the trauma. Her daughter would come home from school every weekend. During holidays, she would encourage Tina to decorate and get involved. "It took me a year to finally forgive myself and 10 years to get over the hate that I felt. I finally accepted after 10 years that it was his mental illness that caused his suicide. I was finally able to open up to God and get out of the negativity that I was carrying in my heart. John, my husband now, was a big factor in my recovery. He is my savior. God works in mysterious ways, he brought us together in the perfect time. John helped me to heal, get over the guilt and connect with my spirituality," said Tina.

"When I look back at the toxic lifestyle that I had with my late ex-husband, I see why things were the way they were. It was his illness. I can finally say it now. I am very thankful for what God has given us. I am thankful to

Sandra, my best friend and Terra, my daughter, for their help. Sandra took me in when he committed suicide and I ended up staying there for six weeks."

Tina now has a thriving income tax and bookkeeping business. She is incredibly helpful to others who are struggling with life's adversities, as she has a heart of gold and an understanding of how difficult life can be sometimes.

If you would like to connect with Tina, you can reach her at tinapauls@bellnet.ca.

The Magic Within

*Stop rushing,
Life is infinite,
It is always moving,
It goes around,
There are always possibilities,
Pay attention
And they will appear.*
- Joany Gauvreau

Joany

I have known Joany for approximately 8 years now. When I met Joany, I instantly knew that I was supposed to have her in my life. I have had this feeling many times and I always acted on this intuition because it has never failed me. I have spoken of Joany in my book a few times. Joany has been an inspiration to me in many ways. She follows her heart and her dreams. When I see her following her dreams, it brings tears of joy to my heart and she inspires me to do the same. Since meeting Joany, I have learned to love my body more by the art of belly dancing. Joany is an amazing teacher and if you ever get the chance to watch her perform, she will move you with her gift of dance and movement. Joany and I share the most beloved treasure, our grandson.

Joany grew up with substance use in her life. This had an effect on how she viewed and responded to the world around her. Joany recalls feeling depressed during her teenage years and having body image issues that led to bulimia and anorexia. Joany made several attempts of suicide via overdosing. She drank regularly and to an excess to cope with her life. She was sexually abused on several occasions when drinking at parties. In her later teens, she was brutally raped. Due to this, Joany slipped into a deep depression and slept for two months. All she did was sleep and eat. She rarely went out and isolated herself from life. Deep sadness and hopelessness overcame her being. She could see it in her eyes when she looked in the mirror. It was as if her spirit had disappeared.

Joany slowly started to go out again. However, her life did not change, as she continued to drink heavily and spent her time partying. She met up with an old boyfriend and spent time with him in attempt to regain her social life.

Later on, Joany was concerned about some physical problems and went to her doctor. He did some tests on her and reported that she was pregnant. Not only was she pregnant, but also she was 8 months pregnant!

Joany was in a complete state of shock, as she could not believe that she was pregnant and not aware of it. Especially 8 months pregnant, that only gave her one-month to prepare for a baby. Joany also feared for the health of her baby, due to her drinking and smoking.

Joany gave birth to an absolutely beautiful and healthy baby girl. This baby was an angel and miracle in Joany's life.

Joany stopped drinking after she became aware of her pregnancy and she has not drank since. Joany described it as a second chance for her. She changed everything about her life, including her eating habits, her thinking and behaviours. She became a fitness instructor and began her new life with her precious baby.

Even though Joany's life had improved, she still felt shattered inside. She went to counselling, treatment for co-dependency and took medication. Low self-esteem lingered as Joany moved from one dysfunctional relationship to another. Joany had a love for teaching fitness and continued to do what she loved despite opposing opinions. As time went on, life took a toll on Joany and she ended up leaving her job as a fitness instructor and went to work in an office environment.

Joany fell into a state of depression again and started eating to cope with her sadness, so she ended up putting on weight again. She never gave up though. Instead, she put up affirmations at her cubical with her intentions for a better future and read them regularly.

One day, Joany found a book on belly dancing, and it enticed her. So she picked it up. Joany started learning the belly dance movements and she found her femininity. She felt beautiful for the first time in her life. When she did the fluid movements, she would cry. She believes now that these circular and figure 8 movements opened her chakras and connected her with her body. The more she danced, the more she loved her beautiful body and she lost over 70 pounds. She found a spiritual healing and connection to her body in her belly dancing. One day, a friend told her that she needed to share her love for belly dancing with others. Joany thought about it and decided to teach and share her talent.

She began to teach and it became more and more successful. A community of women came regularly to learn to dance from her. She also performed in the community and was interviewed by radio and television. Joany started to attract positive and good people into her life. She then met her life partner, Leo. He is supportive and loves her unconditionally.

Joany decided that she wanted to buy her own building and expand her business. She bought a building and worked hard at having it renovated. She spent a lot of money preparing for her business. She expanded and strived to make her business a success. Eventually, it started to unravel and things she had in place fell apart. Joany desperately wanted this to work out, but it didn't matter what she did, it did not work. She began to feel sad and overwhelmed. One day, she decided to go to church and find answers. She went in and sat down at the back, then picked up a weekly brochure. She looked down at it and in bold letters it said, "GET OUT OF THE BUILDING!" She instantly knew what it meant and went home and showed her partner. He was in shock. She then went to the bank and made arrangements to declare bankruptcy. This event was difficult for her, as she had worked so hard at her business. She put her heart and soul into it. Then she took a break with her partner and went to Cuba. While in Cuba, Joany realized that she had to continue to dance and teach. She made the decision that she was going to figure out how to do that. When she returned, she rented a space and started to teach again.

One day, she was getting a massage. All of a sudden, she had a thought that she needed to go to a place in town called Lancelot for apartment rentals. She went in and ended up renting a small apartment in town that was right on the lake.

That led to her seeing a rental space across the street at the mall. The next thing she knew, she was up and running her business again in an amazing location. Joany followed her heart and intuition and her life magically fell into place.
Joany has read and studied the law of attraction and spirituality. When struggling, she would find her inner light by dancing. She describes it as a flame that keeps her going. She now has a thriving business and she continues to work with other artists in similar fields. Joany is also studying to be a life coach, so she can combine coaching with her dancing.

Words of wisdom from Joany:
Ask the universe,
Grant me something that I would love to do.
Be open to anything,
Work through your fear,
Sometimes the unknown is the best thing.
When it feels good inside, you know it is your purpose.
Go after it with unbending intent.

Share it with others, as keeping it to yourself is no fun. Enjoy life.

You can reach Joany at www.feminicity.ca, joanybellydancer@gmail.com and www.femonlinedance.com.

It is in our darkest hour that we have two choices,
To be swallowed up,
Or to reach down to the extraordinary
That is in each one of us and rise above to the
Grandeur that is our destiny.
- Carla Harmer

Carla Harmer

Carla has been a lifelong friend of mine. During my life, she has always been there for me through good and bad times. When my Dad died, Carla was one of my angels who guided and helped me through the difficult days. Her love, compassion and support were always available for our family and we will always be grateful for her presence in our life. My best friend, who I cherish and love with all of my heart, shares her story of hope and strength. Thank you for being my wings, when I could not fly.

I love you, my beautiful spirit friend.

Carla describes herself growing up as a sensitive child. Carla always had an underlying sadness that she could not explain. She now realizes that her sadness was not due to an unhappy childhood, but to the fact that she was extremely sensitive to the pain of other people. Carla had the ability to see other people's auras and to feel their emotions. Hence, she would take on the emotional pain that other people emanated. Due to this, she felt lost and alone as a child. She also didn't realize that not everyone had this extraordinary ability.

When Carla became a teenager, she experienced some abusive relationships with male partners. As a result, she experienced trauma symptoms. She felt like her life was spinning out of control. She could not settle in one place, therefore, she would flee from one place to the next. Carla felt exposed and lived in constant fear of being re-victimized. Crowds were terrifying and her only thought was, "How can I escape if I need to leave?" At home where she felt safe, she would have outbursts of anger and rage in attempts to deal with the underlying fear that plagued her life.

Carla remembers having to wear a mask and persona of always being okay. This led to perfectionist behaviours that manifested into constant concern for her appearance, which resulted in regimented dieting and exercise, excessive working and cleaning her house.

Carla fell in love and her relationship was blissful. She felt happy for the first time in a very long while. However, her perfectionism became rampant and extreme to the point that she felt exhausted and overwhelmed.

After the birth of her son, Carla experienced postpartum depression. She recalls lying on the bathroom floor and sobbing to the point that she could not speak. Her concerned husband asked her what was wrong and all she could do was whisper, "Take the baby to your Mom's house." Carla believes that much of her depressive symptoms were due to sleep deprivation. Due to her perfectionism, she had severe difficulty as a new Mom. When her baby cried, she felt like she was not a good Mom and could not comprehend how she would be able to do this important job. She felt completely empty, as if when she delivered her son, something else left her. She explained that she got through this time with the support of people assisting her with her son. She would walk with her baby, and she sought out counselling and took medication.

Carla also shared that she had traits of co-dependency. These behaviours exasperated her depression and anxiety symptoms. Her need to control and manipulate others was apparent. She would rescue and take responsibility for others as a means to take the focus off of herself. She felt like her life was out of control and she would numb out and cope by eating, work, and television. She didn't realize that by numbing out her perceived negative emotions, she was also numbing out her positive emotions as well.

Carla's depression peaked when her body went into a near state of catatonia. Carla describes this experience as her body systems started shutting down. She felt paralyzed physically and emotionally. She felt like her body, mind and spirit had completely closed off. She had to take time off from work for the third time in a desperate attempt to heal.

The Turning Point:
My friend Cindy was in North Bay visiting her friend Irene Dolata. Irene is a colon hydro therapist and she also has resources for nutritional and supplemental aids. Cindy told Irene that I was having a difficult time with depression. Irene asked me to come over to her clinic and see her.

"When I walked into the door, Irene handed me a container with juice in it and said, 'Drink this.' I obeyed her and drank it, as I felt that I had nothing more to lose. Irene then explained to me that this drink had all of the nutrition that my body needed to live and that it would help me to feel better. She sent me home with a box of the juice and I drank it every day. Within a week, I was cleared to return to work. I felt amazing, like my brain woke up due to having the nutrients that it needed to function. Wow, what a miracle. I then realized that prior to meeting Irene, I had broken down and prayed at a deep and profound level. In desperation, I asked for a miracle, as I was completely hopeless and tired of this disorder taking over my life. The ironic thing is the drink that she gave me was from "the miracle tree, moringa oliefera!" This changed my life in such an incredible way that I decided to become a distributor, so that I could share this miracle tree with everyone who would listen. I felt alive again as I had a purpose. Irene and I became best friends and I started meeting new people.

As time went forward, I became aware of how my co-dependency traits were adversely impacting my life. Irene encouraged me to go to treatment for co-dependency at the Camillus Center. I decided to go and face my demons. This experience was very enlightening for me. I came to the realization that I was an enabler and that my behaviours were affecting everyone around me.

I had to take responsibility for my own thoughts and behaviours. I came to the conclusion that the way I was living was not conducive to a healthy lifestyle. Wow, what an incredible eye opening experience. When I returned home, I made significant changes in my life.

During this time of change, I had everything in my life stripped from my job, identity, money, my relationship and me. The treatment that I had gave me strength to continue forward. My spirituality was enhanced and I felt divinely inspired. I opened up and surrendered to a new way of living. I started working the 12-step program. I realized that I had to give up being a victim. What a realization! I had played the victim for many years. I find that it is very easy to slip back into this mentality. It is important for me to have the assistance of my supports and a sponsor to monitor my thoughts and behaviours. This helps to keep me accountable to my new life and future goals.

Through learning about energetic work, I have been able to protect myself from taking on the energy of other people. These techniques have been very helpful for me when I am in situations where I may be susceptible. I used to feel like a sitting duck getting bombarded by negative energy coming at me from all directions. I would internalize other people's moods and feel responsibility for them. I am now aware of this and I work through it, instead of reacting and taking on their energy.

It has been a huge journey of discovery for me and I am still learning more everyday about this life and myself. I am so grateful for my family and friends, who have been there to support me and walk beside me, holding my hand when I needed it. I am eternally grateful for my Higher Power and the answers I have been provided with to enhance my life journey. My family and I now live in harmony. We all celebrate our life together daily and I am happy and content."

Carla has written a book describing her journey living with depression. She also speaks to groups as a motivational speaker to assist others in their own journey. Carla is spreading her hope, joy and inspiration to the world. She is a beautiful spirit and her light will assist in positively impacting the consciousness of the world.

Here is an insert from Carla's book, *Chasing Light, Finding a Way Out of the Shadows*.

In the light of this new day, I say to myself, "This is the day."

Today is the day I do it. Whatever "it" is, it is up to me. I can grow and change, or I can stay as I am.

Why wouldn't I take the opportunity of this new day and use it to serve the greatest good?

Today, I will rise to the occasion to serve my highest potential.

I deserve to be all that I can be, reap the rewards and all the gifts the Universe has planned for me.

I understand that in order to live my best life, I must fuel my body with healthy food, exercise, fresh air and positive affirming thoughts.

I must connect to the part of me that is God through quiet moments, and loving my family and friends to the best of my ability.

Today I am strong and capable with an amazing capacity for greatness.

Today is the day!

You can reach Carla at www.carlaharmer.com or email her at carla.harmer@gmail.com.

Recognize your Soul's passion as your life destiny.
When you know yourself, you then find your power.
You become that medicine.
You know who you are.
You know your breath.
- Pam Tremblay

Pam

I have only known Pam for a short while. Pam is one of those people who you meet and within a short time, they carve a positive outcome in your life. Pam has overcome many painful obstacles in her life and she has risen to be a powerful healer and woman of incredible wisdom. I saw a picture of Pam on Facebook and I could see in her pictures, her shining light and love towards humanity and our mother earth. I messaged her as a stranger and explained to her my intuition about her and asked her to meet me for coffee. Pam agreed and today we are now friends. Here is her amazing story.

"By the time I was five, I had lost all connections from my relatives, friends and community. My mother had gathered her four children to start a new life away from her husband and father of her children. He had become a chronic alcoholic with mental health disorders. At this tender age,

I became lost in a strange environment, confused, alone and scarred. So began the journey.

As an adult, my life started to unfold around self-discovery and healing, when I found the part of self called Spirit. I had searched for answers through the church, but that did not work. I had learned a lot on this path, but was not finding my way, nor my healing. The effects of childhood and teen traumas were still well and alive in my psyche and body.

As an evolving adult, I went from relationship to relationship, which included two marriages. My son left at the age of 15 and vanished for 8 years, only to resurface at the age of 23, an addict, mentally and physically in anguish. Needless to say, my very long chapter of a mother's grief, depression and being riddled with feelings of guilt and helplessness transformed into another form of grief and guilt. I tried to help, but it was not what he was looking for. So the journey continued with my own experiences, and being what I felt to be a helpless witness to my son's journey, while still dealing with my own wounds and challenges.

I believe that my most profound and true growth and healing began once I discovered Native Spirituality.

Knowing that I myself was aboriginal, the draw and calling of this path was stronger than desire. It was fate. I felt pushed by Inner Spirit to discover my own sense of resilience, which I saw in my own mother. I felt myself rising above the deep murky waters from the results of past traumas, depression, emotional numbness and unhealthy relationships.

I re-learned (I say re-learned, because we all have this in us) how to fully engage in a relationship with nature and began to know how to love myself and to see my true self. I continued to push my way through the pain, fears and loneliness inside me. I sat often in nature, participated in sweat lodge ceremonies, where I felt safe and un-judged, and trusted that the Spirit of the Water that came in my dreams was there to help in my healing.

I discovered my 'voice' through ceremony and truly understood that God (Creator) was not separate from me, but was found all around and in me. I remembered reading one day, that God (Creator) is found in a Blade of Grass. An Elder told me that Creator (The Great Spirit) is everywhere and in everyone. My eyes were opened and I found myself. I realized that my long-lived drive, both to continue to live and to give, came from within and also from my experiences.

The pieces of my life's puzzle were all coming into place as I maintained hope and self-respect. By persevering and not giving up on life and myself, I finally found the Inner Power that I had been hearing and reading about. It was real and alive, not only in me, but I saw it in others.

We all have something to live through. We all have mountains to climb. They may not all be the same, but never the less they are there. We all have been given tools and abilities to go on, to seek, to discover, to heal and to grow.

One of the things that I have come to see is that The Spiritual Path is not a thing. It is acknowledging and honouring one's Inner Spirit. It is a way of being and in the being, we are not alone.

Today, I continue to heal, discover, and grow. By acknowledging my wounds and practicing self-forgiveness, I am able to forgive others. I council others in an Aboriginal Healing Program. I teach from knowledge and accumulated wisdom based on my own experiences at any opportunity that is placed on my path. When someone asks for help, I help to my fullest, while remembering my own sometimes fragile yet very strong

Spirit, and frequently give workshops on Creativity and Art as Medicine.

"On the path of recovery, I learned how to love my self and others, as well as discovering how to live a true and joyful life." Pamela Tremblay

Pam can be contacted at pamsoulsister@hotmail.com or pamtremblay55@gmail.com.

Everything is love,
It is the most powerful energy in the universe,
Love yourself and everything around you.
- John Hayes

John

John has been in our lives for a short time. He is an inspiration to us and he has helped us through some difficult times using his alternative approaches. The work that he does is very powerful and spiritual. We are both so grateful to have such an incredible man in our life.

John was a drinker at an early age. He started drinking regularly at age 12. By age 16, he had a serious drinking problem. He knew he had a problem and he often wondered why none of his family or friends helped him. Drinking made him feel good and he felt like he could become someone else under the influence. When John was sober, he was a quiet person. Due to his family upbringing, drinking and violence became normal to him.

John joined the military as a teenager and he served in Vietnam. His experience during the war resulted in major symptoms of PTSD and grief.

One day at the age of 42, he was in a bar talking to a friend and told his friend that he felt that he only had a few weeks to live due to his disease of alcoholism. When John recollected this, he disclosed that he didn't care at the time if he lived or died. Ironically, during this conversation a man came out of nowhere in the bar and said to him, "If you want to quit drinking, call this number." Then he handed him a piece of paper with a phone number on it. For some reason, he called the number and it was the first step on his journey of recovery. The strange thing that he shared was the fact that this man came out of nowhere, almost like he walked through the wall. Also, no one knew or had seen this man before or after. John now believes that he was a spirit guide who had come to help him on his path to wellness.

John went to a detoxification center and then a residential treatment center for 6 months following. He became a sober man, but severe depression plagued him for the next 15 years.

He recalls sitting with a gun in his mouth wanting to pull the trigger, but for some reason he didn't. Suicidal ideations tormented him for years and sadness reined over him like a black cloud.

His younger brother then died at the age of 49 due to alcoholism. This death rocked John's world and an empty feeling grew in his gut. The death of his brother, even though it was painful, was something that he needed to move forward with his life. He then moved north and began to work with an aboriginal man. He re-embraced his aboriginal culture and began attending sweats on a regular basis. When John came out of the sweats, he would gasp for air. However, the more often he practiced the sweats, the more his gasping decreased.

He believes that this was a symbol of his healing journey. As time went forward, John became immersed in the cultural practices. He worked with his inner child and this was life changing for him. He described this experience as the more he connected with his inner child; his inner light also became brighter.

John believes that we all have an inner power and as long as we keep it in a positive energy, it will protect you. He also has learned healing practices, which have been instrumental in his healing journey.

He now shares his native culture, spiritual practices and story with others. John has daily rituals that offer gratitude to his Creator and his motto is to love, respect and be kind to others and to Mother Earth. John works alongside his life partner in aboriginal traditional healing, shares his strength, hope and love. John is an Elder who counsels, and helps people heal through his story telling and drumming.

He believes that a person has to have a healthy fear of their addiction in order to stay sober. This will assist in the person doing what they need to do daily to walk the path of recovery and healing.

John makes an eloquent statement of his life journey:
"I am who I am today because of who I was yesterday,
I will be who I am tomorrow because of who I am today."

You can reach John at gilwedin@hotmail.com.

The Magic Within

Life is not about what you have done in the past
Or what has been done to you.
Life is about what you do today
And letting go of the past.
Do not let the ghosts of your past haunt your present.
              -Alan Wade

Alan's Story of Change

As a kid growing up in the late sixties and seventies, I was very adventurous. I would get into trouble, just like every other kid does when they are ten or eleven years old. One day, I went into the local church where I lived. I really do not remember my age due to burying the whole experience as deeply as possible. Yes, I was not supposed to be in the church, and yes, I got caught there. I remember this hand grabbing me from behind and the man shook me like I was a rag doll. A quick shot to my head and I was in no condition to put up any fight. I remember being dragged and partially walking to a room. I could hear a fierce voice that said I deserved to be punished for what I had done. It did not make sense, as I had really done nothing. I just went in to look around. I remember having my pants pulled down and being spanked, but then something totally terrible happened. The pain was overwhelming, because I had just been sexually assaulted. I remember him grabbing me afterwards and virtually dragging me outside where he pushed me off the stairs. Then he said that I would go to hell if I told anyone or if I ever came back. I ran and ran. I did not understand what had happened. I just knew I did not want my parents to know what had happened, because I would get into trouble.

I never told anyone what had happened, literally no one at all. As time went by, I even tried to forget what happened. That did not work as well as I hoped. I had nightmares and struggled with fear. It was not till years later that I realized what had happened to me. I became angry, ashamed and I even blamed myself for what happened. That was my life for a long time. I got mad for small things that happened. I struggled with creating healthy relationships with others. Sure I had friends, but I always felt like an outsider. I had terrible thoughts, and I hurt people in fights. My parents did try having me go to counselling in my early teens, but I was not accepting of talking about it.

There were times when I just wanted to die. I just wanted the pain to go away. I even tried twice to kill myself before I turned 19. That did not work. I was very lucky.

I was in my twenties and things were almost out of control. I was lucky no one was permanently hurt. I hid my pain in drugs and alcohol. It was when I was around 27 years old that I realized I needed to start changing my life or I would not have one for long. I met someone and they helped me to look at life in a different way. This was just a step in the right direction.

Today when the memories of that day come, I get the feeling of total fear. It now only happens for a second, because I have been able to deal with it in a healthy way.

My real saviors were my two kids. They gave me something to work towards and the drive to live my life. Unfortunately, I was just not ready for the relationship with their Mom. I was still not ready to love anyone unconditionally. I could do that for my son and daughter, but not anyone else. We separated but ended up staying good friends until I got married years later and was an idiot to my ex-girlfriend. Life is very funny. I fought with my ex really for the first time. We did not even talk for a few years.

When my marriage came to an end and I had nothing at all, my ex-girlfriend, the mother of my children was right there to help me start over. In fact, her whole family helped me by giving me furniture, support, but most of all, forgiving me for being an idiot.

What happened next are the last few pieces of my life changing for good. I quit my job that I had for twenty-six years and lived with my stepson and my two kids. Just so you know, I have two-step kids that are my ex-wife's kids. They are just a little older than my kids. I never call them step kids, because in my heart, they are my kids. It was because of these four kids that my life changed. My oldest daughter gave me her love. My oldest son gave me his wisdom. My younger son gave me his humor and my younger daughter gave me her strength. From them, I got the courage to change my life for good.

It was amazing, that this big tough guy that really feared nothing and that could survive or do anything was saved by four kids. Life is very funny. Living with the kids was one of the best times I ever had.

If you want to know more about how I overcame the trauma I suffered, go to our website www.themagicwithinseries.com to learn some of the methods that I used to change my life for good. There you can also find some tips on dealing with other traumas that you may have suffered from in your past. You can also contact my coauthor or myself and we can set up some time to talk about healthy changes. Just go to our website, www.themagicwithinseries.com, and leave us a message.

The Magic Within

"You do not drive your car
just looking in your rear view mirror,
So why do you live life looking at your past?
Look at where you are going,
not at where you came from!"

- Alan Wade

Chapter 10

Learning to Be True to You

Learning to be true to you is the most important statement of this whole book. It all starts with you. This means that you are the one who has to do the work and make positive changes in your life. In order to do that, you have to consider yourself important, precious and worthy of an amazing life. Why not you? Just think about this for a minute. What are you teaching your children when you honour yourself? We teach others how to treat us on a daily basis. Other people know if we honour ourselves. They can tell by the way that you behave and interact with them. Show the world that you respect and care about you.

Becoming your own best friend is a great way to get started with being true to yourself. How can you become your own best friend? First by taking good care of yourself and improving your self-talk. Look in the mirror daily and say,

"I love you." If you have difficulty doing this, then you have work to do on this topic.

One of the most important things that I have found in my practice and being a Mom is teaching others to listen to their intuition. Your gut will never lie to you, but your head will. You gut is your connection to your spirit. Sometimes you may get a bad feeling about something without any real evidence of something being wrong. Your mind steps in and questions your gut. In the end, you keep doing whatever you were doing at the time and end up regretting it. I have learned to trust my gut, even when things appear to be all right.

I think of my gut/instinct as similar to animal's instinct. Animals know things. They trust their instinct without any doubt. Because we have a mind, we doubt our instinct. Start paying attention to your gut and listen to it. The more you listen to it, the stronger it will become in the future. This is your 6th sense; it is a gift to you. But this gift only works if you listen to it and make friends with it. After all, it may just save your life someday.

Once you start paying attention to your intuition and following it, you will also notice that the universe is always speaking to you. Pay attention!

I have found that when I pay attention, solutions will appear in a conversation with a friend, a song on the radio, a truck going by with a word on it, or in an article you read. This has happened so many times for me and I knew exactly what to do.

I believe that our loved ones can communicate with us from the spirit world. My Dad has sent me many messages. One message that was the most powerful for me was when I met Alan.

My Dad sculpted bears and other animals from wood and he would use marbles for the eyes. One thing that I realized after he died was that a marble would show up out of nowhere when he was trying to get my attention. I was meeting Alan for the first time. I had a good feeling about him, as we had spoken at great length many times on the phone, but meeting him was different.

I was nervous and excited at the same time. When I first laid my eyes on him, I noticed that he had a unique necklace on. I asked him what was enclosed in the leather, as it was very intriguing. He replied, it is a marble and I made it myself. I then knew that my Dad was telling me that Alan was the one for me. We are still together today and the most amazing thing that Alan did was make me a necklace like his to show me that my Dad is always with me. Now that melted my heart. What an incredible man!

Expect good things to show up in your life. The key word here is EXPECT. Remember how I spoke earlier about what you think about expands. What if you expected good things every day? Wow, what an amazing life you would have! Why not expect good things?

Ask yourself this question. Is it because you think that you don't deserve good things? Maybe you think that the world is not a friendly place, so good things won't happen to you. What if the world shows up the way you expect it to? What if you have that much power? You do! That is the power of your mind! The power of your emotions, vibration, and expectation! Just try it for a week. Wake up every day and say I expect good things to happen today and I am going to write down at the end of the day all of the gifts that came my way.

What do you have to lose? Be like a child again and allow life to be wonderful and brand new.

I liken this to expecting miracles in my life. Miracles happen every day, why can't they happen to you? Sometimes you may end up being a miracle for someone else, and you might make his or her day. You have no idea what an act of kindness maybe for someone else. You are a miracle. Once you start to believe that, then your life will change. You are an amazing human being. Notice I said human, BEING, not human doing. What are you BEING? Choose what you want to be – either happy, joyful and kind, or sad, negative, and angry. Decide today that you are going to choose who you are going to BE. Only you have the choice.

When we start changing our thoughts, behaviours and expectations, our life will change. This takes practice and work, because our behaviours and thoughts will not change overnight. Be patient and kind with yourself. Be gentle and keep moving forward. Never ever give up.

My father's tragic death was difficult for my family and we miss him very much. I will never understand why or how this happened. I have decided that I have to stop living in the past and learn from the event. I have realized how precious each moment of each day really is. We never know when it will be our last day or the last day of someone we love. Don't miss an opportunity to tell someone how much you love and adore him or her.

Look at every moment as if it may be your last and cherish it.

Remember, everyone dies, but do we really live? (Quote from movie Braveheart)

Don't have regrets, live life to the fullest. Embrace that magical part of you. Be the powerful creator that you were born to be. Don't wait one more minute. Life is too precious; you are too precious!

There are many people who are suffering from many afflictions and our hope is that these people find the peace and serenity that each person deserves.

THE MAGIC WITHIN is going to be a series of books that will focus on different subjects, all with the purpose of helping as many people as possible. We wrote this book so that you could see what two ordinary people could achieve. If you take what you have learned in this book, you too may achieve something you never thought would be possible.

Stay connected by visiting our website www.themagic withinseries.com. We will be updating our website regularly with information to assist in your healing journey.

We intend to infuse hope in the hearts of everyone's life that we touch and inspiration to follow your hearts desires and dreams.

You can connect with us via our website.

We are available for seminars and speaking engagements.

If you would like to speak to us on a personal basis, you can also reach us via email and let us know your request.

themagicwithinseries@gmail.com

Alan Wade & Cindy Preston

Our website also has bonuses for you to access as part of this series.

www.themagicwithinseries.com

The Magic Within

Life is a journey.
Sometimes the way is clear,
And sometimes it is stormy.
Stay calm and you will find your way.
Listen to your spirit speaking to you.
It is there.
It is real,
And it is a magic space.
That space is yours
To use in stormy times.
They will come and go,
But your spirit will always be.
You will always
BE,
So just BE,
And you will always find your way home.

- Cindy Preston